CULTIVATING
A THOUGHTFUL FAITH

Edited by
Maxie D. Dunnam and Steve G. W. Moore

Cultivating a Thoughtful Faith

Essays by

Paul W. Chilcote	George G. Hunter III
Maxie D. Dunnam	Steve G. W. Moore
Steve Harper	Howard A. Snyder
Ben Witherington III	

Abingdon Press
Nashville

More on *A Thoughtful Faith*

"The title *Cultivating a Thoughtful Faith* aptly describes this book's intent—to develop a thoughtful faith in the lives of believers. Today's Christians need critical, theological thinking. Maxie and Steve have collected the wisdom and experience of great contemporary teachers to provide stimulating thoughts on how we think, speak, act, and live our beliefs today."

George H. Freeman
General Secretary, World Methodist Council
Lake Junaluska, North Carolina

"What a presentation of the need and essence of a well-developed faith, ready for fresh delivery to the impatiently waiting twenty-first century soul!"

David W. Holdren
General Superintendent, The Wesleyan Church
Indianapolis, Indiana

"In a world filled with meaningless rhetoric, *Cultivating a Thoughtful Faith* is a welcome and instructive voice about how the church should be speaking into the culture."

Greg Ligon
Director, Leadership Network
Dallas, Texas

"*Cultivating a Cultivating a Thoughtful Faith* is a practical guide to learning how to make our Christian faith relevant in the midst of a postmodern era. Maxie Dunnam and Steve Moore have compiled articles that challenge each of us to become conscious of how we integrate our theology into our everyday lives and live out a holistic faith."

Amy Lerner Wasserbauer
Primary Therapist, Remuda Ranch
Wickenburg, Arizona

CULTIVATING A THOUGHTFUL FAITH

This book is printed on acid-free paper.

LIBRARY OF CONGRESS CATALOGING-IN-PUBLICATION DATA

Cultivating a thoughtful faith / edited by Maxie D. Dunnam and Steve G. W. Moore; essays by Paul W. Chilcote . . . [et al.].
    p. cm.
    Includes bibliographical references.
    ISBN 0-687-33303-2 (binding: adhesive lay-flat : alk. paper)
    1. Thought and thinking—Religious aspects—Christianity. 2. Theology. 3. Christianity—Philosophy.
I. Dunnam, Maxie D. II. Moore, Steve G. W. III. Chilcote, Paul Wesley, 1954-

    BV4598.4.C85   2005
    230—dc22

                                                                                                        2005021022

05 06 07 08 09 10 11 12 13 14-10 9 8 7 6 5 4 3 2 1
MANUFACTURED IN THE UNITED STATES OF AMERICA

CONTENTS

ACKNOWLEDGMENTS

I have come to believe that gratitude is more of a spiritual discipline than a sign of good manners or benevolent emotion. More and more I am realizing that the idea of self-made people is as much of a myth as new ideas. While there are many people to recognize and thank for this project, it is important to understand that the conception of this book came about initially as a means of honoring Maxie Dunnam for his years of service and leadership at Asbury Seminary. Maxie, as is his fashion, quickly turned the project into something that would honor others and serve the church.

This collection of essays is designed to help guide people in the cultivation of a thoughtful, intentional faith. It is written to dispel the myth that theology is of little use to those wanting a vibrant, alive, contagious faith. An important underlying theme is one that is distinctive to the Wesleyan tradition. It is the idea that faith is both a matter of the heart and the head. It is the belief that what we believe is as important as how our faith makes us feel and live. I hope this book both honors and nurtures that tradition and those who have gone before and those who are to come.

Special thanks need to be expressed for the board of trustees at Asbury Theological Seminary, which first cast the vision for such a project and supported its development. We would like to thank Harriett Olson and John Kutsko for picking up on the vision and casting it even wider. Behind the scenes were many people who worked to edit, type, research, and support this effort. They include Kevin Dean, Joseph Nader, Sheila Lovell, and Harry Zeiders. There are others who are simply champions of encouragement including Paul Baddour, Thanne Moore, Jerry Dunnam, Bill Johnson, Elroy and Vicki Wisian, the Tammys, and many others too numerous to name. We also want to thank the contributors, those who read manuscripts and gave helpful input and critique, and those, like our faculty, who faithfully and regularly nurture and cultivate thoughtful faith in our students and in the lives of so many people in so many places.

Steve G. W. Moore
Summer 2005

LIST OF CONTRIBUTORS

Paul W. Chilcote (Ph.D., Duke University) is visiting professor at Duke Divinity School. He has taught in Africa, England, the Methodist Theological School in Ohio, and elsewhere in the U.S. His recent works include *Recapturing the Wesleys' Vision* and *Changed from Glory into Glory: Praying from Transfiguration to Resurrection*.

Maxie D. Dunnam (Th.M., Emory University; D.Div., Asbury Theological Seminary) is chancellor of Asbury Theological Seminary and formerly served as the fifth president of the seminary from 1994 to 2004. Before coming to lead Asbury, he served thriving pastoral charges at Christ United Methodist Church in Memphis, Tennessee, and elsewhere. He has been an active executive in The United Methodist Church, the World Methodist Council, and the Association of Theological Schools. His popular collections of writings include *The Workbook of Living Prayer, Unless We Pray, and Let Me Say That Again*.

Steve Harper (Ph.D., Duke University) is vice president of the Florida campus of Asbury Theological Seminary in Orlando. His teaching specialties of spiritual formation and Wesley studies parallel his ministry focus on nurturing Methodist pastors and congregations. His previous titles include *The Way to Heaven: The Gospel According to Wesley* and *Devotional Life in the Wesleyan Tradition*.

George G. Hunter III (Ph.D., Northwestern University) is distinguished professor of communications and evangelism and formerly the founding dean of the E. Stanley Jones School of World Mission and Evangelism at Asbury Theological Seminary. Among his recent books are *The Pastor's Guide to Growing a Christlike Church* and *Radical Outreach: Recovery of Apostolic Ministry and Evangelism*.

Steve G. W. Moore (Ph.D., University of Michigan), a leader in Christian higher education and spiritual formation, is senior vice president of

Asbury Theological Seminary and president of the Asbury Foundation for Theological Education. He previously served as a vice president at both Seattle Pacific University and Baylor University. His forthcoming titles include *College 101: A Guide to Getting the Most Out of College* and *The Legacy Project: Presidential Leadership in Christian Higher Education*.

Howard A. Snyder (Ph.D., University of Notre Dame) is professor of the history and theology of mission at the E. Stanley Jones School of World Mission and Evangelism of Asbury Theological Seminary. Snyder maintains an active schedule of speaking at conferences. His current teaching interests include missiology, church renewal, and globalization. His latest titles include *Decoding the Church: Mapping the DNA of Christ's Body* and *The Community of the King* (revised).

Ben Witherington III (Ph.D., Durham, England) is professor of New Testament at Asbury Theological Seminary. His expertise includes the role of women in the early church, Christology, and Johannine literature. A much sought-after speaker and prolific author, his recent works include *The Brother of Jesus* and commentaries on the books of Romans and Revelation.

THEOLOGY AND A THOUGHTFUL FAITH

Steve G. W. Moore

We are all theologians, whether we want to be or not. We all have ideas about God, how God works, what God has had to say, how God might want us to live. Our collection of ideas about God, however organized or disorganized it may be, represents our theology. The question is not if we are theologians or not, but are we good theologians or bad theologians? It is helpful to ask ourselves, "Are my ideas about God accurate? Where did I get these ideas? Have others had similar ideas?" Ideas have consequences. Good theology should lead us to living well. Bad theology can lead us not only to incomplete living, but it can also lead to flawed relationships and a less-than-fulfilling life.

Of course, none of us have it all right. We are all theologians in process. We each must make it our life's purpose to intentionally be growing in our understanding of God, how God is working, how God is inviting us to join in the divine work, and how God desires to work in and through us.

Theology matters. Ideas matter. For most of us, life is so hurried it is hard to imagine the luxury of having time to think about such supposedly esoteric matters as theology. But the truth is that good theology is very practical, very down-to-earth, very everyday-ish. Good theology is not pie-in-the-sky, ivory-tower philosophizing. Good theology is the stuff of life. Two stories from the Gospels help us to see this fact.

Do you remember the time a young man approached Jesus and asked, "What does it take to inherit a life forever with God?" We are told that he was rich. If he interpreted wealth as a sign of God's blessings, then he may have assumed—before asking Jesus the question—that God already had reserved a spot for him in heaven. Or he may have thought that he could somehow buy a way into heaven by giving large offerings in the temple or maybe that God would require just a portion of his wealth be given to the poor. In any case, he was obviously shocked by Jesus' answer, for when Jesus said, "Sell all you have," the rich young man became sad (Mark 10:21-22 NLT). We get the sense that Jesus' straightforward statement caught him off guard. Jesus has a way of doing that.

We are told of another man who was a smart guy. He came to question Jesus about which of the 613 or so Jewish commandments was the greatest. He undoubtedly was quite knowledgeable about the biblical laws and religious traditions. He was not only asking Jesus a theological question—he was also asking Jesus a priority question. Though we do not have the benefit of hearing the tone of his voice or seeing the expression on his face, we get the hint in the text that he was asking a trick question in an attempt to trap Jesus. "The most important one," answered Jesus, "is this: Hear, O Israel, the Lord our God, the Lord is one. Love the Lord your God with all your heart and with all your soul and with all your mind and with all your strength. The second is this: Love your neighbor as yourself. There is no commandment greater than these" (Mark 12:28-31 NIV). My guess is that this wise guy thought he already had his theology all worked out and that he expected to teach Jesus a thing or two. We are told, though, that after Jesus' answer, no one dared to ask Jesus any more questions.

These two brief encounters tell us at least four very important things pertinent to theology and a thoughtful faith for everyday life:

- Good theology always begins with God.

- Good theology is not just about our mind; it involves all of what it means to be human—our thoughts, emotions, and our physical body.

- Good theology guides and instructs how we relate to the world and all of the people around us.

- Good theology is foundational to the way we live our lives, how we view our time on earth, and the hope we have for when we leave this earth.

Often, professional theologians organize their work in specific ways. For example, they may include topics such as who God says God is, why

God created the world, and how God desires to interact with it. Theology considers what causes the problems we face in our world, the solutions to those problems, and what we are to expect from God in this world and later. It has been my observation that some people's theology focuses all their ideas and energies around what they understand to be the fastest, most efficient way to get to heaven. Others are anxious about how to keep people from slippage, rust, damage, or theft of their souls before they get to heaven. Such people construct a theology concerned with warehousing the soul until one is heaven bound—usually by an elaborate list of prohibitions. Still others think theology is about righting all the wrongs in this world or revealing all the ways people are doing bad theology!

The point here is that all of those ideas represent people doing theology, but doing it in incomplete ways. The challenge we face as we seek to nurture a thoughtful faith is to be open enough to grow and learn, but confident enough to stand fast. Meldenius, a Christian leader from an earlier century, gave some very helpful wisdom about cultivating a thoughtful faith when he said, "In essentials, unity; in nonessentials, liberty; in all things, charity." He was encouraging an attitude of humility and certainty, openness and hospitality—all to be held together at the same time.

There is an important distinction we should also point out early on in our seeking to develop a thoughtful faith. Sincerity, while an admirable and desirable characteristic, is never a test of truth. One of the clear lessons of history is that people can be sincerely (and often tragically) wrong. The hijackers who flew the planes into the World Trade Center were very sincere. But they were sincerely misguided. Their theology had consequences of tragic proportions. Their sincerity was linked to bad theology, flawed ideas about God and God's will for our world. The ripple effects of that event are still being felt. Ideas—good and bad—have consequences. Theology has consequences.

We certainly want to encourage and cultivate sincerity, genuineness, openness, and honesty. But we want to ground these traits in that which is true, good, and beautiful, and integrate them on a daily basis in down-to-earth kinds of ways.

Annie Dillard, a Pulitzer Prize author reminds us:

> How we spend our days is, of course, how we spend our lives. What we do with this hour, and that one, is what we are doing. A schedule defends us from chaos and whim. It is a net for catching our days. It is a

scaffolding on which a worker can stand and labor with both hands at sections of time.[1]

We are building our theology every day. Every day, our actions reveal what we actually believe and prioritize in our lives—even as our credit card statements and appointment books reveal what we truly value. Moreover, our everyday actions, as they harden into habits of the heart, can affect and alter—for better or worse—what we believe.

Christians of every educational level, social standing, and career path are called to be thoughtful followers of Jesus. Every day we have opportunities to act with forethought by allowing our actions to be guided by our theological beliefs. What we believe about Jesus should affect how we treat our neighbors. What we know about the good news should change our lives. What we experience in the living church should inspire our living out the faith. Our actions ought to reflect what we believe as Christians.

In this volume, we seek to provide a chorus of voices to inspire our living, instruct our thinking, and encourage a more thoughtful faith. In each chapter, you will find ideas and images woven together in the hopes of helping you to love the Lord with all of your heart, soul, mind, and strength and to love your neighbor as yourself.

AN ENCLAVE OF RESISTANCE

Maxie D. Dunnam

Spirituality begins in theology (the revelation and understanding of God) and is guided by it. And theology is never truly itself apart from being expressed in the bodies of the men and women to whom God gives life and whom God then intends to live a full salvation life (spirituality).
—Eugene H. Peterson,
Christ Plays in Ten Thousand Places

In September 2002 there was a formal blessing and dedication service for the new Cathedral of Our Lady of the Angels in Los Angeles. Unlike the European cathedrals of old that took generations to complete, construction crews took only three years from the time of excavation in 1999 to build this cathedral out of 151 million pounds of materials. The structure is designed to withstand an 8.0 magnitude earthquake and is expected to serve for five hundred years.

Located in the heart of downtown Los Angeles, the eleven-story structure stands along the famous Hollywood Freeway, one of the most heavily traveled freeways in the nation. So, like the ancient cathedrals, this one also sits in the midst of the hustle and bustle of the city. To create a space for prayer on this very public site, famous Spanish architect José Rafael Moneo was commissioned.

Moneo says he wanted to create "buffering, intermediating spaces," such as plazas, staircases, and colonnades. His creative, modern design used almost no right angles. The resulting complex geometry creates unexpected, mysterious spaces for worshipers.[1]

One *Los Angeles Times* journalist commented, "Moneo is creating an alternative world to the everyday world that surrounds the cathedral, a testimony to grandeur of the human spirit, an antidote to a world that is increasingly spiritually empty." Then he wrote this sentence: "The cathedral, set in the midst of the secular city, will be an enclave of resistance."[2] Consider this image: the church as an enclave of resistance.

My friend Mark Trotter once preached a sermon in which he suggested that enclave should be a part of the mission statement of every congregation: "an enclave of resistance against all that diminishes human life."[3] Whether or not this word should be a part of every congregation's mission statement is not my concern in this essay. That *enclave* should be a factor in our awareness of who we are as the church is absolutely crucial.

Let me state the relevance of this last thought for the Christian community and for institutions of theological education in particular. A big part of my calling from the pastorate to become president of a seminary was the conviction that *as the seminary goes, so goes the pastor; as the pastor goes, so goes the local congregation; as the local congregation goes, so goes the whole church.* Theological schools, if their mission is to teach, train, and equip persons for ministry in the church, lose their way if they fail to keep a clear vision of the church.

The church is not our idea, but God's. God called Israel in the days of Moses to be God's people: "You shall be for me a priestly kingdom and a holy nation" (Exodus 19:6). The call of the church in the days of the apostles echoes this identity: "You are a chosen race, a royal priesthood, a holy nation" (1 Peter 2:9). Jesus was clear about the church's identity. His church would be built on the faith commitment that Jesus was the Messiah, Son of the living God (see Matthew 16:13-20).

Everything that a Christian community does—the way it orders its life as a group, what it teaches (and even how it teaches), how and why it expands its mission, in essence, its whole life and purpose—must be evaluated by how well it lives up to the church's holy identity and foundation on Jesus. As a graduate theological institution, a seminary or divinity school must be judged by this question: how is the church being served? Questions about the nature of the church—its life and ministry, its unique expression in present culture—should be a significant part of the dialogue within a seminary. It is because of these convictions that the image of the church as an enclave has kept a grip on my mind for several years now. So, here I share some of my reflections.

BEING AN ENCLAVE OF RESISTANCE

Let's begin by thinking about the nature of resistance. In one of my favorite Charles Schulz's *Peanuts* cartoons, Lucy demands that Linus change the television channel.[4] She even threatens him with her fist if he doesn't listen:

Why do you think you can just walk in and take over, Linus questions Lucy.

These five fingers, replies Lucy. Individually they may mean nothing, but when curled together they form a weapon that is terrible to behold.

So which channel do you want? asks Linus. Turning away, Linus looks at his fingers and says to them, Why can't you guys get organized like that?

The church has never been able to get organized in its resistance to the world. In fact, the church has never been able to understand consistently what it means to be *in* the world, but not *of* the world. Yet in every period of history, the church has known that its very nature provokes some form of resistance. There is always the sense in which kingdom ideals or norms are in conflict with the realities of cultural contexts in which the kingdom exists. How the church should relate to the world has been debated throughout history. This conflict has been expressed in different ways.

We should not be surprised that theological revisionists attempt to order mission and ministry on the conviction that the church's task is to respond and adjust to the world, not try to convert it. On the contrary, we do not need to adjust to the world, we need to convert it. Scripture is diminished, even denigrated, in this stance of adjusting because priority is given to listening to the world without the crucial reference point of first listening to the Word of God.

As God's faithful people, we are sometimes called to resist the forces that drive the world. The witness of people like Dietrich Bonhoeffer, who paid dearly for his convictions, must never be lost from memory.

3

Bonhoeffer's words ring on in clear opposition to those who would adapt rather than seek to redeem culture:

> The Church is always on the battlefield . . . struggling to prevent the world from becoming the Church and the Church from becoming the world. The world is the world and the Church the Church, and yet the Word of God must go forth from the Church into all the world, proclaiming that the earth is the Lord's and all that therein is.[5]

Resistance, then, is a part of the church's proclamation and the center of our demonstration. We resist the moral relativism operative in our society. Yet we embrace new ways to speak to our culture. This is no easy assignment: how do we encourage thinking while simultaneously monitoring our boundaries? As Steve Harper says later in this volume, "I am growing in the conviction that the primary role of theological education is not to teach students what to think, but rather to guide them in how they think. As well, it is about the formation of an alive dynamic faith and the shaping of who we become as persons and not just about ideas, propositional truth, or shaping the 'mind.'"

In other words, we resist the moral relativism prevalent in our culture.

Off and on throughout history, strong movements have arisen that emphasized denying the world—an action that hints at a monastic retreat from life or withdrawing from the world as much as possible. As a member of the holiness movement, I can say the following: though we would not readily acknowledge it, the holiness movement in Wesleyan circles has a close affinity to the monastic movement. It has a marked world-denying dimension. To affirm the world and to celebrate and enjoy what our world has to offer is difficult for "holiness people." In our attempt at holiness, we make the *world* our enemy, when the truth is the world is evil only when we become its slave.

A second perspective that has often prevailed is the notion that we must wage war with the world. In recent times this notion has been expressed most dramatically in what cultural observers and the media call the "religious right" (especially the radical right). The argument has been that Christians need to take over the government. The problem with this view is that in any governmental system, some human being has to be in a place of power. So, we put our person on the throne. We soon learn how much power corrupts, and how true it is that absolute power corrupts absolutely. When will we learn that we cannot establish the kingdom of God before the King comes? Any sort of war against the world is basically an effort to set up a kingdom without a king.

Another perspective, a third way besides reactionary retreat and a will to power, does exist. Throughout history we've been at our best when we have heard the message of Jesus that we are to be salt, leaven, and light; we are to bring people into relationship with Jesus Christ, a relationship of love that is powerfully transforming. It is this vision of being salt, leaven, and light that best fits the biblical image of the church being an enclave of resistance.

The question is not whether we are in a war or not. We are at war. Paul was certain of this fact. He defined the nature of the war in which we are engaged in Ephesians: "For we are not fighting against people made of flesh and blood, but against the evil rulers and authorities of the unseen world, against those mighty powers of darkness who rule this world, and against wicked spirits in the heavenly realms" (Ephesians 6:12 NLT).

Too often we see ourselves at war with human powers or with the flesh. Thus, we use the weapons and ways of the flesh to wage our war as though that were the arena of battle. Paul says we battle not against flesh, but "principalities" and "powers" (as the King James Version puts it). He also announces in Colossians that Christ has already won the battle: Jesus has "disarmed principalities and powers" and has "made a public spectacle of them" (Colossians 2:15 NKJV).

Our stance must be that of persons who are clear about who the real King is and confident that the King is the victorious One. We seek, then, to live as the Kingdom has already come, and to live as the salt, leaven, and light of it. The Christian community, therefore, becomes at least a hint and glimpse of how things ultimately will be when King Jesus establishes his rule completely.

We always need to be careful about the nature and focus of our resistance. We must not deceive ourselves into thinking that if we can get the right king on the throne—elect the right president, the right Congress, the right governor, and put our people in places of political power—then we can win the battle. There can be no kingdom without a king, and the kingdom to which we're committed has only one King—Jesus. The church needs to think more of transformation than of confrontation. We need to think more about long obedience in the same direction than about quick fixes that may bring superficial changes.

Our task as an enclave of resistance is to subvert the calloused, materialistic, secular culture of which we are a part. We can subvert that culture at its roots by living as though we believe that we do not live by bread alone, as though there is a kingdom reality of love, as though the imperatives of

5

Romans 12 are operative: Our love is without hypocrisy. We abhor what is evil and we cling to what is good. In honor we give preference to one another. We are able to rejoice in hope. We are able to be patient in tribulation. We attend to the needs of the saints. We give ourselves to hospitality. We bless those who persecute us. We rejoice with those who rejoice. We weep with those who weep. We associate with the humble. We do not see ourselves as wise in our own opinions. We don't repay evil for evil. We seek to live peaceably with all persons. We feed our enemies and give them drink. We overcome evil with good.

Any community living out this kind of love is a counterculture. In this kind of living, there exists a power within the Christian community that would subvert the foundations of all that is contrary to the kingdom of Christ. Let me give this some specific shape as we ask the question: how do we, as an enclave of resistance, subvert culture at its root through transformation rather than through a stereotypical against-the-world tactic?

THE HOLY CHURCH OR NO CHURCH

I want to paint with broad strokes in the following paragraphs. This statement from John Wesley reminds us of the peril in which we stand:

> I am not afraid that the people called Methodists should ever cease to exist either in Europe or America. But I am afraid lest they should only exist as a dead sect, having the form of religion without the power. And this undoubtedly will be the case unless they hold fast both the doctrine, spirit, and discipline with which they first set out.[6]

Christian communities have the tremendous responsibility of holding fast the doctrine, spirit, and discipline with which they first set out. I suggest that the model for that endeavor is an enclave of resistance—a church that is holy, charismatic, and apostolic. I know these are loaded adjectives, charted with diverse meanings. But what I want to articulate is that the church needs a synthesis of Wesleyan theology, charismatic experience, and an apostolic vision for the mission of the church.

Of this, Howard Snyder made the case that the scriptural portrait of the church is both holy and charismatic.[7] I doubt if there is any greater need than for us to recover our dual nature of holy and charismatic. Both are pressing concerns.

There is no question in either Scripture or Wesleyan sources that the community of faith is to be a holy people. Our commitment and passion have not always matched the demand. Certainly the Methodist/Wesleyan movement as a whole—as well as other denominations and movements—has strayed from this center. Oftentimes, outsiders of a movement have better insight than insiders into what is wrong with a movement. Methodist bishop William Oden once told of a visit with Gustavo Gutiérrez, the father of liberation theology. Oden was eager to discuss theology; Gutiérrez wanted to discuss Methodism. The bishop wanted to hear about Gutiérrez's lay academy in Lima, Peru, and his being silenced by Rome. Gutiérrez wanted to talk about his Methodist friends Mortimer Arias, Emilio Castro, and Justo Gonzáles.

"Tell me about Methodism in America," Gutiérrez said.

"We are struggling to find our center," Oden responded.

Gutiérrez looked at him. "You already have a center."

"Share it with me," the bishop implored.

This is what the theologian shared:

> It's scriptural holiness. You inherited that center from Wesley. Don't you see that scriptural holiness is the exact word needed today? Wesley's theology of holiness comes out of the merger of a theology of creation and the experience of God's grace. The holy earth and the holy life cannot be separated.

Shaking his head he continued,

> Holiness has been reduced to neurotic perfectionism by some. It's not. It is the joyous response to the grace of God. Holiness is the movement of both creation and church toward fulfillment in God's love. Wesley called it "Christian perfection," and he organized his movement to be small cells of nurture and growth to that end.

Their time up, Gutiérrez embraced Oden and concluded, "Friend, if Methodism can keep its center, it will be a faithful force for God. If not," he shrugged his shoulders, "God will raise up another community with the same biblical and theological vision."[8]

Can we in Methodism hear that prophetic word from a Roman Catholic priest? What distinguishes a Methodist? Holiness of heart and life does. If we could recover that holiness within the Wesleyan movement, then the church would become an enclave of resistance. How do we recover holiness? Listen to another word from Mr. Wesley:

If you preach doctrine only, the people will become antinomians; and if you preach experience only, they will become enthusiasts; and if you preach practice only, they will become Pharisees. But if you preach all these and do not enforce discipline, Methodism will become like a highly cultivated garden without a fence, exposed to the ravages of the wild boar of the forest.[9]

We are seeing the ravage happen. The wild boar of the forest has been loosed in the highly cultivated garden of the Wesleyan movement—and in all mainline denominations for that matter. Many in the church are accommodating the ways of the world rather than resisting its ways and seeking to redeem the people lost in the world. Our lack of holiness betrays, even annuls, our call to orthodox faith. Moreover, we are forgoing discipline within the church to the point that even bishops (in The United Methodist Church, Episcopal Church, and perhaps elsewhere) can't hold each other accountable. So, Wesley's warning that the Methodist movement could become a dead sect is an ominous possibility, certainly in the United States.

Holiness is a joyous response to the grace of God. Only as we recover the transforming dynamic of holiness will our proclamation of God's grace be heard by others. Only by holiness will the church thrive as an enclave of resistance.

Ezekiel the prophet made clear why our holiness is so pivotal. The prophet says that God's honor must be restored in the sight of the nations. Israel had profaned the covenant God had made with her. As a result, pagan powers were allowed to carry God's people into exile. But God gives a glimmer of hope: "The nations shall know that I am the LORD, says the Lord GOD, when through you I display my holiness before their eyes" (Ezekial 36:23). The world will not pay attention to the church until those of us who call ourselves God's people vindicate God's holiness before their eyes.

The path of holiness is a precarious one. Here I will outline some principles we need to keep at the center of our awareness. The first is this: holiness, by its very nature, is an enemy of the relativism pervasive in our culture. Francis Schaeffer has spoken a challenging word at this point in his *The Great Evangelical Disaster*: "If our reflex action is always accommodation, regardless of the centrality of the truth involved, there is something wrong. Just as what we may call holiness without love is not God's kind of holiness, so also what we call love without holiness is not God's kind of love."[10]

8

A second principle we need to keep in mind is that obedience is the operative word for holy living. Oswald Chambers never ceases to be challenging and probing: in one of his devotions he says, "The golden rule for understanding spiritually is not intellect, but obedience. If a man wants scientific knowledge, intellectual curiosity is his guide; but if he wants insight in what Jesus Christ teaches, he can only get it by obedience."[11] The overarching principle is that obedience is essential for holy living. When we talk about holiness we are talking about:

Discipline—not legalism
Conviction—not intolerance
Sacrifice—not asceticism
Freedom—not bondage
Joy—not misery

THE CHARISMATIC CHURCH
IS THE NEXT CHURCH

The church as an enclave of resistance will not only be holy but also charismatic. By "charismatic" I mean that the church came to birth through the Spirit; thus, the church lives and functions by the Spirit. Theoretically, no one would disagree with this conviction. Functionally, however, we do disagree. Where is the mainline (or even classic evangelical) denomination that incorporates that conviction as a core principle for ordering congregational life?

The charismatic nature of the church underscores not only a dependence on the power of the Holy Spirit for life and sustenance, but also an ongoing expectation of a Spirit-empowered community. While in some communities the existence of love may be deemed miraculous, in a Spirit-empowered community the people can anticipate the following behaviors as normative: love, mutual care, forgiveness, healing, reconciliation, restoration, deliverance, social witness, and the breaking down of barriers (e.g., racial, economic, social). The congregations I know in the United States who are the most vital—winning the most people to Jesus Christ, abolishing social barriers, bringing diverse people together, freeing people effectively from drug addiction, helping care for the poor—are those who at least in some dimension know themselves to be charismatic. Beyond the United States, several recent observers of the world Christian movement (including Philip Jenkins in *The Next Christendom* and Edmund W. Robb in *The Spirit Who Will Not Be Tamed*) have noted that the fastest growing congregations and movements in Asia, Africa, and South America are largely charismatic. The church that does not pay attention to its intrinsic charismatic nature will be far less than God's dream for it.

The seminary that does not assist the church in appropriating the reality of the Spirit-empowered life will have failed in the servant role. For example, the mission statement of Asbury Theological Seminary is "to prepare and send forth a well-trained, sanctified, Spirit-filled, evangelistic ministry" to spread scriptural holiness throughout the world.[12] It was not happenstance that the founding president, H. C. Morrison, put *sanctified* and *Spirit-filled* together in this statement.

What an enclave of resistance the Church would become if these two crucial dynamics were realized: holy and charismatic, in the best meaning of both of those words.

THE APOSTOLIC CHURCH BUILT ON MACEDONIAN COFFEE

Add now a third dynamic to being an enclave of resistance: apostolic. It must see itself from an apostolic perspective.

Several years ago Richard Halverson, former chaplain to the U.S. Senate, described the evolution of the church in this way:

> In the beginning, the church was a fellowship of men and women who centered their lives in the living Christ. They had a personal and vital relationship with the Lord and it transformed their lives and the world around them. But then the church moved to Greece, where it became a philosophy. And then it moved to Rome, where it became an institution. And then it moved to Europe, where it became a culture. And now it has moved to America, where it has become an enterprise.[13]

What an indictment: the church as a philosophy, an institution, a culture, an enterprise. Any of these violates God's intentions for the church. It is to be a fellowship of people who have a vital and personal relationship with the Lord that transforms their lives, and as a result, becomes an enclave of resistance to the surrounding world.

Let me offer a picture from outside American culture—this may inspire our thinking about the apostolic nature of the church. The picture comes from my work with World Evangelism of the World Methodist Council. Imagine these scenes: For days on end, a trucker has been driving between Bulgaria and Albania. His eyes are burning, he struggles to keep the vehicle on the road, he's tired, and he needs sleep. He pulls over into a rest area and falls asleep. In a home nearby, very early in the morning, while the truckers are still sleeping, a wife gets out of bed, makes coffee, and pours it into pots to keep it hot. Her husband, a Methodist minister in Macedonia, heads to the truck stop with the coffee. He taps on a window and awakens the trucker. As a minister of the Methodist Church, he shares a cup of coffee in the name of Christ. The trucker eventually becomes a trusting Christian. In the driver's home village of Tsenowo in Bulgaria, there is no church. He travels fifty miles to find a Methodist congregation in Russmae. With the assistance of the pastor of that congregation, a new Methodist congregation begins in Tsenowo. That's apostolic!

How we understand ourselves as the church and how we perceive our cultural setting will determine the shape of our life and witness. The apostolic nature of our time calls us to give more attention to:

Appreciating Scripture as revelation and authority;
Practicing apologetics;
Creating and sustaining Christian community;
Leading and empowering laity;
Forming Christian identity and character in a secularized culture;
Building a critical relationship with culture;
Understanding technology;
Developing the language and resources for worship;
Experiencing faith rooted in Scripture and tradition, yet freed
    from hindering customs and unnecessary cultural strictures.

Let such a church arise—holy, charismatic, apostolic. Only such a church—an enclave of resistance—is going to be the powerful kingdom, yet humble servant witness, to challenge the principalities and powers holding sway in our age. Our call is to help create such a church. If we do so, the Lord will call us blessed, and that is the only reward we seek.

THINKING AS AN ACT
OF WORSHIP

Steve Harper

*The Church exists to be the light of the world, and if it fulfils
its function, the world is transformed in spite of all the obsta-
cles that human powers place in the way. A secularist culture
can only exist, so to speak, in the dark. It is a prison in
which the human spirit confines itself when it is shut out of
the wider world of reality.*
—Christopher Dawson, *The Criterion*, October 1934

He was one of my students, and I liked him. But when he submit-
ted his term paper, I was surprised to discover that the only foot-
notes he included were taken from the Bible. There was no
evidence whatsoever in the paper that he had used any other source.
Given that he was a graduate student in a theological school, I had to call
him to my office to see what was going on.

When I pointed out the problem to him, he didn't flinch. Instead, he
told me that while he was in college, a professor-mentor had told him
words to this effect, "You may read anything as a Christian, but when you
are expressing your convictions, you must only use the Bible." He had
accepted that counsel. Consequently, it was a short step from absorbing

his mentor's philosophy to applying it in his research papers. He was at a place in his life where establishing fundamental thoughts could only occur through the use of Scripture. Fortunately, this is the only experience like this that I have had in nearly twenty-five years of teaching. The incident reflects a mind-set, however, that I see expressing itself in other equally bothersome ways.

After more than two decades of teaching seminary students, I am growing in the conviction that the primary role of theological education is not to teach students *what* to think, but rather to guide them in *how* they think. Long after their textbooks have gone out of print and their notes have grown cold in a file somewhere, they will be living and ministering every day out of the capacity to think about and think through all sorts of principles and practices. The ultimate challenge is not to fill the mind, but to *cultivate* it so that a lifelong journey of Christian thinking can be set in motion. That is what I want to address in the short span of this essay: What does it mean to *think* as a Christian?

DESIRE

One day Jesus was approached by a lawyer from the party of the Sadducees who asked him, "Teacher, which commandment in the law is the greatest?" (Matthew 22:36). Jesus ended up giving two commandments that were very close together, but in the first he included the commitment to love God with our *mind*. The very first thing to notice here is the linkage between the notions of *love* and *mind*. Our modern concept of love has become so overly emotional and sentimental that we hardly even see a mental act as an expression of love. When it comes to loving God, we easily can include attitudes and actions that may be linked with passion and/or compassion, but we do not include so easily what we would call the more intellectual dimensions of our lives.

If we are going to *think* like Christians, we must begin by recognizing that our fundamental desire must be to love God with every aspect of our being. We must see that good thinking is as much a part of loving God as is anything else. Our desire to be devoted fully to God cannot exclude any dimension of human life. Moreover, it is our new life in Christ that provides the basis to direct our thinking, keep it within proper limits, and save it from pride.[1]

This comprehensive desire is at the heart of our discipleship. The essential meaning of the term *disciple* is to be a *learner*. In other words, our desire to love God manifests itself in a disposition to be a learner all our days. The words of the old hymn summarize our desire "to see Thee more clearly, love Thee more dearly, and follow Thee more nearly—day by day."

If my student had viewed life in this way, the whole world would have become a classroom from which he could draw from anything and everything to learn more about God and God's will for his life. Every subject that honors Christ and edifies life becomes a source for our growth in grace. This is nothing other than what the psalmist had in mind in the declaration, "The heavens are telling the glory of God; and the firmament proclaims his handiwork" (Psalm 19:1). This perspective fuels a lifelong desire to enrich our thinking from a wide variety of options.

DESIGN

We quickly come to see that desire by itself is not enough. There has to be a design to which our desire is attached, and it makes a great deal of difference what that design is. Our experience in the Internet world is sufficient to prove the point. When we do a search online, we are almost always given an immediate and immense number of hits. The problem is, we usually are not given any direction as to the relative importance of the selected sites, except for the frequency of use. There is no wisdom in the ordering of the results; we only know them in order of descending popularity. It doesn't take long to realize that this can be a misleading differentiation, if not a dangerous one.

Thinking requires a design. Everyone thinks according to some kind of design, even if it is largely unconscious. For Christians, that design is Christ. When we ask ourselves, "Why Christ?" our response is simply that Christianity arose because of one particular life. We cannot live the Christian life or hope to *think* as Christians apart from a profound attachment to him. I believe this was the notion communicated in John 15, and it has been the dominant view in the Christian tradition ever since. Thomas Oden has captured the thought in his systematic theology: "The meaning of Christianity is undecipherable without grasping the meaning of Christ's life and death and living presence."[2]

At this very point we take a decisive turn in the development of Christian thinking. Even if we agree that Christ is the design, we must acknowledge that our understanding of him is mediated through a progression of Scripture, early church sources, medieval sources, Reformation writers, and modern interpreters. Oden calls this mediation the Pyramid of Sources, with the Bible at the base and the modern authors at the tip.[3] This fact alone should have altered the view of my student, who was living with the mistaken notion that he could form his convictions with an exclusive linkage between what he read in the Bible and the effect it had upon him. He did not realize that twenty centuries later, we are the products of this progressive process. Yes, Christ is the design, but none of us has arrived in isolation from a thoughtful reflection on what that means and where our formative influences have fit into it. To say it another way, when we *think* as Christians, we do so within both the context of two thousand years of distinctive Christian development and the Old Testament environment that preceded it.

Because this is an essay on the subject of Christian thinking, we are at the point where we must limit our idea that Christ is our design to the more specific question of "How did Christ think?" What follows is not an exhaustive answer to that question, for I am not able to provide that kind of response. The elements of the design for Christian thinking, as taken from Christ, are limited to those things which stood out to me over the years as I pondered that question.

First, Jesus thought as a person of his time. When Luke 2:52 states that "Jesus increased in wisdom and in years, and in divine and human favor," it is the New Testament's way of saying that Jesus participated in the educational system of his day. Deuteronomy 6:1-9 charged parents with the responsibility to teach their children. Consequently, the home was the first and most effective agent in the educational process. At the core was the teaching of religion. But much more was taught than that. Trades were passed on through apprenticeship. Domestic skills were transmitted. A general life orientation was provided. At the right time, the synagogue came alongside the home to teach subjects like reading, writing, and arithmetic—as well as further dimensions of religion. All this is to say that as Jesus developed his way of thinking, he was doing so within the context of the culture, not apart from it. Jesus learned within the educational and cultural context of his day, as Merrill Tenny, Lawrence Richards, and others have pointed out.[4]

Second, Jesus thought with a transcendent orientation. The goal of education was not the mere acquisition of knowledge, but rather growth in godliness. For Jews, education was one of the means to foster holy living. When the previously quoted verse in Luke refers to "divine and human favor," it is the mixture of heaven and earth which was the aim of education in Jesus' day. We can only imagine that Jesus' facility with such things as parables was cultivated within an educational formation that had taught him to see God in all things.

The pages of history are replete with stories of people engaged in Christian thinking who consciously seek to find the transcendent in the temporal. George Washington Carver, for example, was able to see God in a peanut, and he did more to unlock its uses than any other person. The "Apostle of Literacy" Frank Laubach saw God in teaching people how to read. Mother Teresa saw God in one dying man who did not need to die alone. Your own life may contain illustrations of how you have been enriched in your relationship with God by developing a similar consciousness.

Third, Jesus thought with the intention to transmit what he knew. The purpose of education in his time was not for the student just to become smarter, but for the student to become a teacher. When Jesus began and practiced public ministry, he was never averse to being called *teacher*, and he welcomed the title *rabbi*. Jesus understood that central to his mission was the mandate to transmit what he had received. In many ways, the rest of the New Testament is commentary on the gospel that was incarnate in Jesus and communicated by him.

If my student had only realized that he had *never* learned from the Bible exclusively, he would have been a lot better off. If he had realized that, like Jesus, he was the product of a much larger educational system, he would have felt a freedom to use that system to his advantage—and to do so fully within the context of faith. Because he had forgotten to remember and give thanks for all of his teachers, he had come to seminary with a view of education which Christ himself did not hold. As we now see, there is still more to Christian thinking than either our desire to do it or the design we're given for it.

DEVELOPMENT

Christian thinking is thinking like Jesus—at least that's our working definition in this essay. For that to be true, there must be the cultivation of what the Bible refers to as the mind of Christ (Philippians 2:5-11). This thinking is more than the accumulation of facts; it is the development of a way of looking at life and appropriating truth from life. Dennis Kinlaw has described the Christian mind this way: "To have 'the mind of Christ' is to have His perspective, His attitude, and priorities."[5] This idea has had a great impact on my life.

First, to develop the mind of Christ is to have a particular sense about life. This sense means we understand fully and deeply that the meaning of life does not reside within us. Paul described Christ's mind in these words: "Though he was in the form of God, did not regard equality with God as something to be exploited" (Philippians 2:6). Jesus was the Son of God, the Second Person of the Trinity. Yet, in his humanity, Jesus did not live as if he were equal with God nor as if he did not need God. Instead, Jesus demonstrated a healthy dependency upon God. The Gospel of John makes this model clear in many places.

Likewise, we do not take the fact that we are made in the image of God as permission to live independently from God. We live with the sense of being connected to the Center, but we never *are* the Center. We live with a healthy dependency upon God, always drawing our lives and getting our guidance from God. Furthermore, we never outgrow this sense of life, but rather we carry it with us as long as we live. As a result, we think openly and receptively. We are always learning and growing—but never arriving. Christian thinking is a journey, not a destination.

In this regard, I often tell students that if I could change one thing in theological education, I would change the name of the degree: master of divinity—how presumptuous! We never master divinity. Rather, we are supposed to become increasingly mastered by divinity. Christian thinking is, therefore, always subsidiary to Scripture and tradition, not equal to them, much less above them. Accepting this idea is what produces the right attitude in us. Without this attitude, we may secretly believe we "really don't need to know that"—or worse, we can become disengaged because we think we already know it all. I have had the joy of working with students who understood themselves as disciples (that is, learners), and I have had the struggle of working with students who had deceived themselves into thinking they had all they needed. Christian thinking is an attitude before it is an activity.

Second, to develop the mind of Christ is to make an intentional *surrender* to God. Paul describes this surrender by saying that Jesus "emptied himself" (Philippians 2:7). Following on the heels of attitude is the fundamental activity that must be present if we are to practice Christian thinking. We must be those who surrender ourselves to God in Christ.

We must cultivate the heart and mind of a learner, receptive each day and in all of our experiences to what God may desire to teach us. We are always pupils in God's school. God is always the teacher, and we are always those being taught. The quality of surrender in our thinking creates the humility necessary to learn—the very humility that Paul says Jesus had in his mind (Philippians 2:8).

James W. Sire has written an intriguing book entitled *Habits of the Mind: Intellectual Life as a Christian Calling*. After describing the character of the mind essentially as a passion for truth and a passion for holiness, he moves quickly to describe the spirit which must be present, and that is *humility*: "Without it," he writes, "every virtue begins to become a vice. A passion for truth becomes a certitude that we have found and now possess it. A passion for holiness becomes self-righteousness."[6]

But the lack of humility does more than work against our thinking; the lack of humility ends up putting off others from engaging in Christian thinking themselves. Richard John Neuhaus has pointed out in "Encountered by the Truth," a *First Things* article, that our arrogance creates a barrier which prevents others from seeking what we most hope they will come to know. He writes, "Few things have contributed to the unbelief of the modern and post-modern world as the pretension of Christians to know more than we do."[7] He exhorts Christians to regain the spirit of humility as a necessary means of attracting others to the faith. Do we not hear an echo in this exhortation—an echo for us to have the kind of humility which enables common people to hear us gladly, as they did when Jesus taught them what he knew? Such humility can only come from a surrendered mind—a mind which always upholds the point of view that "You're God; I'm not."

Third, to develop the mind of Christ is to live with a *servant* orientation. Without this orientation, Christian thinking becomes another version of consumerism. Worse, our thinking can become idolatry. In *No God But God*, Os Guinness and John Seel describe the problem in these words, "Idols are not just on pagan altars, but in well-educated human hearts and minds. The apostle Paul associates the dynamics of human greed, lust, craving, and coveting with idolatry."[8] Notice that every word used to name the problem is a term that depicts self-centeredness, not surrender. By contrast, Paul describes Jesus' mind in the second chapter of Philippians as one that took the form of a servant and became obedient all the way to dying on the cross.

Christian thinking always understands that learning is a means, not an end. In the process of our thinking, we always ask ourselves, "What for?"

and "Who for?" This view does not mean we fail to assimilate our learning into our own lives, for that would make us hypocrites. But it does mean that we are not satisfied to merely "know"; we are also desirous to know how what we know can be transferred, and how what we know can be used in the transformation of others.

Likewise, we discover that the servant-mind of Christ will lead us to places of sacrifice. There will be times when we realize that sharing what we know will only lead others to misunderstand and/or react against us. Transmission will sometimes be the most countercultural thing we can do, and we may receive no respect for it whatsoever. But the same passion for truth and holiness which burns within us (cleansing and conforming us more fully into the image of Christ) is the passion that will not let us keep what we know to ourselves. Christian thinking is by its very nature evangelistic. We are always learning and living for the sake of others.

Christian thinking is, therefore, directly connected to prayer. We continually must be asking God to give us the mind of Christ—his sense, his surrender, and his servanthood. We know that Christ's mind is much more than IQ; it is an HQ (heart quotient) that measures Christian thinking more in terms of attitude than amount. Such prayer also will create the final quality that I want to lift up in this essay.

DEPLOYMENT

Christian thinking creates an aroma—a distinctive scent that both verifies its presence and attracts interest in others. As we come to the end of this essay, we need to be careful to deploy our thinking in ways that achieve these ends. In this regard, several qualities will characterize our thinking.

First, we will be *lovers*. We will, as we've previously shown, have a passion for what we think. This passion is the difference between being a reporter and being a witness. Reporters can show up and accurately describe an event they personally have not experienced. Witnesses, however, tell you what they have seen and heard. Witnesses tell the story standing within it, not outside of it. Witnesses have lived the story, not merely documented it.

At the heart of Jesus' life was a profound love for God. As a result, his life became an expression of God's love for the world. Christian thinking is an experience that begins in our love for God and then moves to include our love for others. We hardly ever connect the words *intellect* and *love*, but the Bible understands that they are always together. As we said at the beginning of this essay, the Great Commandment exhorts us to love God with our minds. Christian thinking is an act of love. True intellectuals are lovers.

When I think back to my best teachers, it is easy to see this fact. They were all witnesses. They were all lovers. Sometimes, their love spilled over into moments of emotion and ecstasy. At other times, they showed the love of quiet devotion and scholarly persistence. Now, years later, it is their love and passion that I remember more easily than what they actually taught me. I can go to their books and my notes to remember what they said. But I only have to open my heart to recall that they were lovers. If you are reading this as essentially a student, then let me encourage you to view your thinking and your learning as one of the most profound acts of love that you can give to God. If you are reading this primarily as a teacher, then let me encourage you to instruct others as one who loves.

Long ago, notes James Sire, St. Bernard of Clairvaux captured what I am trying to say as he wrote:

> There are many who seek knowledge for the sake of knowledge; that is curiosity. There are others who desire to know in order that they may be known; that is vanity. Others seek knowledge in order to sell it; that is dishonorable. But there are some who seek knowledge in order to edify others; that is love.[9]

Second, we will be *learners*. We have already duly noted this quality of Christian thinking, but now we reflect on it in relation to how we position ourselves for influence. I have a colleague who gets through to others, partially because he nearly always couches his thinking in these words, "This is only my opinion, you understand." It is not unusual for him to go on to say, "If you have more light on this subject than I do, I want you to tell me." This is not a crafty communication technique (although I have seen it disarm an audience), it is a disposition to further growth. It is a witness to the fact that none of us has a grasp on the whole truth. It is a testimony that often Christian thinking is best done in community, with each person offering what he or she knows.

When I think of this disposition, I think of E. Stanley Jones. His practice of using the round table, as in *Christ at the Round Table*, was a sign of his desire for everyone to contribute the best from their particular religion, philosophy, or point of view. Similarly, when he was asked to name the best years of his life, he almost always responded, "the next ten." He was a learner. He learned from others and he learned through the passing of time. He was never satisfied to stop where he was. He was always reaching out for more.

Underneath his attitude of a learner was a profound belief in the infiniteness of God—how do you ever get to the end of that? What option do we have but to keep learning and growing? Brother Stanley (as he was often called) even believed we would continue to learn in heaven. He just couldn't imagine a static or stagnant reality. To be this kind of learner does not mean we will never have convictions; it means that we will know that convictions (though deep and solid) are always improvable—and the desire to go on to perfection in our thinking will be alive in us.

Third, we will be *lights*. We live in a dark world. As Jesus told Nicodemus, we live in a world where oftentimes people prefer darkness to light. Likewise, Jesus also declared us to be lights to the world—set on a hill with the distinctive mission to give light to others. If we are first lovers and then learners, we do not have to fear that bearing the light will be mistaken as presumptuous and exhibiting a holier-than-thou attitude. No, we will always engage in Christian thinking as those who firmly believe that we have a message the world needs to hear and that it is God's message. We are only the conduits, not the content.

I hope you have had the opportunity to be in the presence of "lights." Beginning in elementary school and continuing to the present, I have had teachers who were lights. They are the Christian thinkers who leave you with a bigger picture of the world than you had before you met them or were taught by them. Another thing about light is that it is not self-referent. Light moves outward away from itself. I have been privileged to know people who want to give rather than take. Thanks to them, I have come to see that Christian thinking is about being a light.

Christian thinking is also stewardship. We have been given a great message; it is not our invention and it is not our possession. We did not write the story, but we have the marvelous privilege of telling it. To do so, we must *think to the glory of God*. We have our most complete example of this in Christ, and we have it further modeled for us in the great cloud of witnesses who both preceded and followed Jesus in the Judeo-Christian tradition. Christian thinking is ultimately an act of worship. It is at the heart of Paul's invitation for us to present ourselves to God (Romans 12:1). But it is also an act which brings great joy to us, for as we engage in it, we find ourselves exclaiming, "For this I was made!"

THINKING THEOLOGICALLY,
THINKING BIBLICALLY
Howard A. Snyder

*When the Christian faith is not only felt, but thought, it has
practical results which may be inconvenient.*
—T. S. Eliot, *The Idea of a Christian Society*

God speaks to us authoritatively through the Word illuminated by the Holy Spirit. Even so, Christians often disagree on what the Bible really *means*. For us to understand what God is wanting to say to us through the words of the Bible, we have to do more than read the words of the Bible. We have to deepen our ability to understand and interpret.

Jesus Christ, the incarnate Word, has left us the sacred Scripture, the written Word, to guide Christians on our course through history and culture. He has sent us his Holy Spirit to help us interpret the Bible in light of Jesus Christ and to understand Jesus Christ in light of the Bible. Jesus said to "search the scriptures," for they "testify" of him (John 5:39). Jesus taught the Word to the two bewildered disciples on the road to Emmaus. In a remarkable statement, we read that Jesus, "beginning with Moses and all the prophets . . . interpreted to them the things about himself in all the scriptures" (Luke 24:27).

This is good news! Yet from the very beginning, Jesus' followers have had trouble knowing how to understand and properly interpret Scripture.

The book of Acts, which is the story of Pentecost and the remarkable growth of the early church, is also the story of the church's struggle with Scripture. We see the apostle Peter, for example, gaining new insight into Scripture through his encounter with Cornelius the centurion. He told the crowd at Cornelius's house, "I truly understand that God shows no partiality, but in every nation anyone who fears him and does what is right is acceptable to him" (Acts 10:34-35). That insight was a new learning for Peter—emotionally, if not cognitively; no doubt he had read as much in the Hebrew Scriptures.

How we interpret Scripture is partly a function of how we think. And how we think is the complex product of temperament, education, and cultural context. Even our genetic makeup likely influences our approaches to Scripture.

Most of us notice pretty early that not everyone thinks alike! Children learn (or not) how to figure out their parents' thinking—and vice-versa. Pastors struggle with the different ways their parishioners think—and vice-versa. Theologians think differently not only in content but also in styles of thought. Is this part of the difference, perhaps between Karl Barth, C. S. Lewis, and Morton Kelsey or between John Calvin, John Wesley, and Martin Luther? Furthermore, do we gravitate toward writers who think the way we do?

The more basic question is this: How do we think biblically and theologically? I suggest here three models that may prove useful. In interpreting the Bible and thinking theologically, we tend to interpret things in one of three ways: *logically, analogically,* or *psychologically.* One could consider a number of other models, but I find this tri-focal lens especially useful for interpreting Scripture and for gaining insight into different theologians and theologies. This approach gives us some insight into how and why we form our beliefs the way we do.

THREE WAYS WE THINK

How do we reach theological conclusions? The answer is not only a matter of the facts and stories learned through Scripture and tradition. Theology is shaped not just by the materials, but also by the tools we use. It is shaped by the way we think—and we don't all think in the same way. People seem to think mainly in one of three quite different ways. Partly because of this phenomenon, we have different views, different beliefs, and different churches. Some of us tend to think primarily on the basis of logic (using reason); others are more analogical (using stories or imagination); and some think more psychologically (using intuition). These ways of thinking are not mutually exclusive; we tend to use all three much of the time and according to context. In most people, however, one approach tends to dominate. Imagine a sort of triangle, like this:

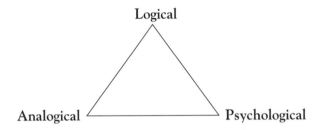

These are different ways people think. I would argue that all are good, and even necessary. One could thus view these as overlapping spheres or circles—a reminder that the three constantly interact with each other.

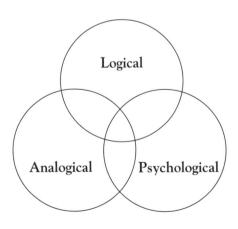

If someone said you are a "very logical person," would you take that comment as a compliment or an insult? Most people living in Western societies would probably take it as a compliment. Because Europe was so influenced by the Age of Reason and the Enlightenment in the seventeenth and eighteenth centuries and by the rich inheritance of Greek and Roman philosophy, Western culture came to place great emphasis on a logical mind-set. But not every culture in the world—and not every person in the West—would consider being called logical a compliment. In some cultures, higher status would be signaled if you were said to be one who "tells good stories" or "just has a sense" (intuition) of what is true or right.

WHAT IS YOUR STYLE?

We will examine each of these styles in turn. This study will help us see what style each of us mainly uses, how that shapes our interpretations of Scripture, and, thus, how we think biblically and theologically.

Logical Thinking

Logic is highly valued in the West, especially in the fields of philosophy and theology and in certain professions, such as law. Logic has wonderful strengths, but it also has some key limitations.

The main human capacity logic uses is *reason*. Logical thinking specializes in propositions that declare what is true or not true. In classical logic, a key tool is the syllogism—a formal way of stating propositions that helps one construct sound logical arguments and demolish faulty ones. A syllogism consists of two statements or premises, then a conclusion drawn from these. John Wesley was very familiar with this way of reasoning. For a while, he taught logic at Oxford University, and throughout his life he enriched his writing with many formal and informal syllogisms.

Syllogisms can be fun, but they're only as good as their premises. They can be either valid or invalid, and they can be tricky.

A valid syllogism would be:

> All normal cows have four legs.
> Bessie is a normal cow.
> Therefore Bessie has four legs.

But this would be an invalid syllogism:

> All cows have four legs.
> Rover has four legs.
> Therefore Rover is a cow.

A logician quickly spots the flaw in the invalid syllogism. The second statement is faulty as a premise because it replaces the more general category (kind of animal—cow or dog) with a more limited one (four legs). All normal cows have four legs, but not all four-legged creatures are cows (fortunately, since cows don't make very good house pets).

Syllogisms can be useful in theology because they help us be precise. Unfortunately they are often abused in theology—either by faulty premises or, more commonly, by simply omitting the second premise but assuming it to be true. For example:

> Christians are saved by faith, not by good works.
> Therefore Christians should not do good works.

This argument leaves out several intervening steps that would need to be examined in order for the conclusion to follow logically from the premise. Theology can be full of this kind of false, or at least questionable, reasoning. A valid syllogism, however, has all the certainty of a mathematical proof. If the premises are valid, the conclusion *has* to be true just as surely as two plus two equals four.

We may call the logical approach the way of classical science, or at least of the scientific method that developed especially during the Enlightenment. Good scientific inquiry is logical. Valid scientific conclusions rest not only on the methods and the experiments but also on the logic that underlies them.

Some of the greatest Christian theologians have been logicians *par excellence*. Thomas Aquinas constructed highly complex arguments. Karl Barth in his great *Church Dogmatics* made extensive use of logic—sometimes using logic even to show its limitations.

Logical reasoning apparently draws more on the left side of the brain than on the right side. Research into how the brain works suggests that logical functions happen more in the left hemisphere and imaginative functions more in the right. Is systematic theology mainly a left-brained activity?

Analogical Thinking

Some people dwell more in the realm of imagination than in the world of logic. Their thinking tends to be more *analogical* than logical—which is not illogical, just different. When we think of analogical approaches, we think of art and poetry. In analogical thinking, rather than using propositions to declare something "is" or "is not," we talk about how something is "like" or "not like" something else; i.e., "My love is like a rose." Or we may use "is" but with the sense of "like": "No man is an island," said John Donne. This is the land of metaphor and simile—and also of story.

The Bible is full of analogical language. Think of Old Testament stories, of Jesus' parables, or David's poetry. Righteous people are "like trees planted by streams of water" (Psalm 1:3). Much of the Bible, in both its history and its poetry, is in narrative form. Good theology, like good preaching, uses analogical thinking. As a boy, Sir Walter Scott once heard John Wesley preach and years later recalled, "He told many excellent stories!"

Some of the most influential theologians and Christian writers of the twentieth century were great storytellers. Think of the Oxford friends, C. S. Lewis, J. R. R. Tolkien, and Charles Williams. It is remarkable how many contemporary Christian leaders such as Charles Colson owe their conversions or their Christian worldview in large part to Lewis's influence. Lewis himself (and the likes of Dorothy L. Sayers) was influenced by the storytelling powers of Williams. Tolkien's *Lord of the Rings* has been immortalized by Peter Jackson's movie trilogy, which exposed a whole new generation in the twenty-first century to the epic tale of good versus evil. If logic is the way of science, analogical thinking is the way of art. The genius of art is the role of metaphor and imagination. Artists will tell you they don't try to picture things as they are, but rather as they imagine them. They are concerned with a deeper reality than what appears on visible surfaces.

A key tool of analogical thinking, along with imagination, is paradox. This seems almost the opposite of the syllogism. Paradoxes stand propositions on their heads by declaring that two seemingly contradictory statements may both be true. Since Albert Einstein's theory of relativity, science increasingly has had to wrestle with paradox, especially in quantum physics. Fritjof Capra and others say scientific investigation is becoming as much art as science. Jesus was a master of paradox when he needed to be, especially when dealing with his critics. Think about the questions he posed about his own identity—"If David thus calls him Lord, how can he be his son?" (Matthew 22:45).

In contrast with logic, analogical thinking draws more on the right side of the brain. New research suggests that there may be physiological influences that contribute to our preferences for logical or analogical thinking.

Psychological Thinking

Finally, there is psychological reasoning. Here the accent is not on reason or imagination, but on emotion—that which deeply moves us. We face here the reality and influence of feelings, moods, and attitudes. Where reason may employ the syllogism and analogical thinking, the paradox—psychological thinking—uses intuition. Intuition, of course, plays a role in logical and analogical thinking, but in psychological thinking it is primary.

In this approach, key statements are not about what "is" or what something "is like," but rather about how things "seem" or "feel." At the end of an impressive logical argument have you ever said, "Yes, but it just doesn't *feel* right"? Or perhaps someone has said to you, "I really can't give my reasons for this, but it seems to me this is the way things really are." That's psychological thinking. Instead of propositions (logic) or stories (analogical thinking), psychological reasoning in more fully elaborated form may use myth or allegory—special forms of story. This is not the way of science or art primarily, but is often the way of games and play. Like analogical reasoning, it draws heavily on the right side of the brain, though, of course, not exclusively.

The Bible is full of psychological insights, and we find numerous examples of psychological reasoning. Several of the Old Testament writers at times use myth and allegory to communicate God's message. And throughout the Bible—in contrast with much of Western culture—we find the prominence of dreams (e.g., Genesis 20; 1 Kings 3; Daniel; Acts 18).

Many of the great mystics and spiritual writers of the church have used psychological reasoning in addition to analogical reasoning. Psychological thinking is found more rarely in systematic theology, which (at least in the West) has tended to value rational thought above all else.

Psychological reasoning often abounds in sermons, however, as pastors try to connect with the felt needs of their congregations or give telling illustrations.

One great master of this approach in the twentieth century was Carl Jung. Though not a theologian or a preacher, Jung has had a huge influence on a number of Christian thinkers and writers such as Morton Kelsey, partly because of his emphasis on the importance of dreams and symbols in understanding our faith and relationship with God.

These three main ways of thinking—logical, analogical, and psychological—are encountered constantly in Christian life and theology. They abound also in Scripture—another testimony of the comprehensive and holistic nature of the Bible. This is a sign to us that we should value all three approaches as we live out our Christian discipleship.

Three Modes of Thinking

	LOGICAL	ANALOGICAL	PSYCHOLOGICAL
Primary Faculty	Reason	Imagination	Emotion
Key words	"Is"/"Is not"	"Is like"	"Seems"/"Feels"
Tools	Syllogism	Paradox	Intuition/"Sense"
Modes	Proposition	Story/Parable	Myth/Allegory
Field	"Science'	"Art"	"Game"/"Play'
Exemplars	Aquinas, Barth	Lewis, Buechner	Jung, Kelsey, Bultmann
Hemispheres of Activity	Left Brain	Right Brain	Right Brain

Recalling the triangle on page 25, we summarize these three modes of thinking in the chart above.

We all combine these different modes at different times and in various situations or perhaps according to different activities that engage us. Yet it seems that for most of us, one mode predominates most of the time. If we think about this phenomenon, we can see that each has a role to play. We need all three in the Christian life, in the church, and in our biblical interpretation.

Who is your favorite doctor? The best physicians are the ones who combine these three modes. They know how to reason clearly and precisely. They can make those more indirect connections that come from analogy and imagination, practicing the art as well as the science of medicine. Plus, they have good intuition and strong empathy. Often they simply sense what is wrong and then are able to confirm this by further diagnosis.

But how often we may think that *our* way of thinking is the *right* way and that other ways are inferior!

THINKING OUT OUR BELIEFS AND DOCTRINES

For Christians, beliefs and creeds are important. We take theology seriously because we know it makes a huge difference in how we live. Saving faith is not just a matter of having faith or believing something. Saving faith is a matter of believing and confessing that some things are true and some things are false. Most important, saving faith is faith in someone—Jesus Christ as Savior and Lord, "For there is no other name under heaven given among mortals by which we must be saved" (Acts 4:12).

But how do we think about what is important theologically—important for our faith and life? A big part of the answer concerns our reading and interpretation of Scripture.

We notice that the Bible is full of stories, as well as of doctrines and history. We tell the stories of Jesus; we recall and teach the stories of Old Testament heroes and villains—David and Goliath, Daniel in the lions' den, Esther and the king. Like the New Testament writers, we draw theological lessons from biblical characters. The church reflects on biblical and historical accounts, and it forms creeds to nail down points of key doctrinal consensus.

Imagine, then, a different sort of triangle or pyramid:

History is what actually happened, so far as we know. *Story* is how we tell, relate, or imagine what happened. *Creed* is what we believe or confess about

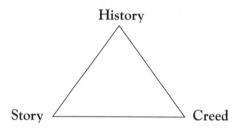

what happened. For example, the apostle Paul wrote, "For I handed on to you as of first importance what I in turn had received: that Christ died for our sins in accordance with the scriptures, and that he was buried, and that he was raised on the third day in accordance with the scriptures, and that he appeared to Cephas, then to the twelve" (1 Corinthians 15:3-5).

Our life is shaped by history, story, and creed—what we believe. All three are very important for Christians, because ours is a historical faith. It makes a critical difference what happened in history—that God created the universe; that Jesus Christ actually lived, died, and was raised to life; that God will fulfill what the Almighty has promised to do in history.

For our witness, it makes a huge difference how we live in history. It makes a difference what stories we *live* and what stories we *tell*. We witness effectively by living and telling our stories in the light of "the old, old story" of what God has done and is doing through Jesus Christ in the power of the Holy Spirit. It is important for our lives and witness what we *believe* about all of this—the key truths of the Christian good news in the context of the actual history of the world.

The question here is, how do we *think* about all of this? And the point is that we don't all think in the same ways, manners, or styles. Whether we think logically, analogically, or psychologically about the history, stories, and creeds that shape our lives determines in significant measure where we come out in our interpretation of events and our understanding of Scripture.

This last point—how we interpret the Bible—is especially critical. What is our biblical hermeneutic (that is, our system of interpreting Scripture)? Is it logical, analogical, psychological, or some mix of all three?

THE DIFFERENCE IT MAKES:
THINKING HOLISTICALLY

How we think makes a big difference. Just as there are values in all three modes of thinking, there are also dangers. How would you like living with a strictly logical person, someone moved only by reason and not much in tune with feelings or emotions? It would not be a very pleasant or livable life. The same would apply for functioning solely by analogical or psychological thinking. People at the analogical extreme might be thought to be "not quite in touch with reality" or "living in the clouds." People at the psychological extreme might be viewed as "not really serious" or "more concerned with feelings than truth."

Clearly, we need a balance. The church needs to take into account all of God's truths when we form our doctrines, and we need to live out all of God's truths in our witness and discipleship.

Clearly, this is an impossible task to do alone; however, it is not an impossible task in community. This is part of the reason God formed the church—to be very literally the Body of Christ in the world, living out the whole, balanced, Spirit-filled life we see in Jesus. We need each other in our thinking and believing, just as we do in our living and loving.

Four practical insights can be drawn from the different ways of thinking discussed here. First, the Church needs to think holistically, combining the logical, analogical, and psychological approaches. We need all three. Each contributes something essential to our lives, our doctrines, and our biblical interpretation.

The Bible teaches that we are created in the image of God. This is a key theological touchstone. In profound ways we as a human race reflect the image of the Holy Trinity: Father, Son, and Holy Spirit. Our capacity to reason and our different ways of reasoning are part of this. Our reasoning gets distorted by sin, just like everything else. Yet we still have the capacity of reason, to be used for God's good purposes and to God's glory.

God, we may assume, thinks holistically. That is, God knows everything that can be known and knows the full length and strength of reason, analogy, art, intuition, and feeling. Theologian Clark Pinnock pictures God not as the "unmoved Mover" but as the "most-moved Mover."

Despite the limitations of our knowledge and ways of thinking, we should try to think like God. This means we should value all three ways of thinking, benefiting from all three. Each contributes something to the other. If we combine these three modes holistically, then our doctrines, our lives, and the church's mission will be more whole, healthy, and entire.

Second, the church needs and should affirm all of the gifts God gives, not just some of them. Paul's teaching to the Corinthian church regarding gifts applies also to our ways of thinking. The church should value and affirm the logical thinkers, the analogical visionaries (some of whom will be prophets), and the psychological thinkers (some of whom will be counselors while others may be ecstatics or have unusual gifts of insight).

How beautiful the church where all gifts are valued and function together to the glory of God and the building up (edification) of the Body of Christ! Churches that value people with these various gifts of thinking styles will be more wholesome and more healing. They will look more like Jesus and be a richer reflection and image of the Trinity.

Remember, too, that the image of God in humanity and in the church is gendered. It exists as male and female. That, strangely and mysteriously but also wonderfully, is God's plan. Historically the church has not sufficiently affirmed or valued the rational gifts of women and has discounted their analogical and psychological contributions. Holistic thinking in the church requires the full and equal participation of both women and men.

Third, the Church needs to build and to be the community of the Spirit. Holistic thinking requires healthy community, and healthy community fosters holistic thinking. The more we are in touch with each other in the Body of Christ—our brothers and sisters in the Spirit—the more we value each other as persons. That action, in turn, leads us to value the different styles of thinking. We are likely to find ourselves saying, "Oh, *now* I see what she means!" or, "*Finally*, I feel like I'm beginning to understand him!"

A key reason the church goes to extremes, and sometimes even divides along the fault lines of different thinking modes, is that it often fails to build real community—holistic *koinonia* (fellowship or community) in the biblical sense.

How did Peter, John, Matthew, Nathaniel, and the other first apostles get along; what about Mary and Martha, Mary Magdalene, Joanna, Susanna, and the many other women disciples referred to in Luke 8:2-3? Well, in fact they often didn't get along—until after Pentecost. Even then they had problems. Paul ran into conflict with Peter, Barnabas, and probably a lot of other early believers. He must have had some interesting conversations with Apollos or with Priscilla in the leather shop in Ephesus.

How did they get along? How did they remain in fellowship and mission? The church progressed by total commitment to Jesus Christ and reliance on the Holy Spirit—and by a strong theology of the church that valued the persons, gifts, and ministries of *all* of the people, with little distinction between men and women, rich and poor, educated and uneducated. They affirmed all of the gifts and recognized that all believers are priests and ministers of the good news.

Finally, considering these three ways of thinking brings us back to the importance of the Holy Scriptures and how we interpret them. Too often biblical interpretation is one-sided or eccentric, depending partly on what mode of thinking is predominant. Overly rationalistic biblical interpretation simply skews God's Word. It needs the balance of other modes. Likewise, hermeneutics often suffers from illegitimate intuitive or analogical interpretative leaps that result in what James Sire calls "Scripture-twisting."

Not every word or promise of Scripture can be legitimately applied to us today. Just because God told Noah to build an ark doesn't mean you and I should start chopping down cypress trees; just because God told Jonah to go to Nineveh doesn't mean we should get on the next flight to Iraq; just because Jesus turned water into wine at one wedding doesn't mean we should expect him to do the same thing at our wedding. These are some obvious examples. More difficult texts require a sound hermeneutic. That means taking the history, stories, and doctrines of Scripture seriously, certainly. It also means combining the logical, analogical, and psychological approaches.

The Bible is amazing. Its holistic message is radical. One testimony to the Bible's Spirit-breathed nature is the remarkable way it combines logical, analogical, and psychological elements. In our interpretation today, we dare not slight any of these.

The Bible is basically a story, a divinely revealed narrative of God's saving intentions and how God has been working these out in history. It projects the story into the future, showing that history is going somewhere—namely, to "new heavens and a new earth, where righteousness is at home" (2 Peter 3:13). Story and history, of course, abound in analogical and psychological elements, as well as logical ones, and we see this clearly in Scripture.

History—especially salvation history—is a rich tapestry of colorful threads that weave together to bring glory to God. Filled with the Spirit, we help weave this tapestry and, in fact, are the threads. If we examine closely, we will see that among those threads are the three we're considering here: logical, analogical, and psychological thinking. We need all three, just as we need each other in the Body of Christ.

Upon reflection, we can ask which of these three modes of thinking has been used in this discussion. Actually I have tried to combine all three. Since this is an essay—a reasoned argument, not primarily a story or a picture or a game—the rational mode is predominant. But I also have tried to also signal the value of the other two modes. To fully appreciate the argument, however, we would need now to expand our understanding by incorporating discussion and fellowship with others.

Retelling the Story in Postmodernity

Ben Witherington III

[L]ess all that we take to be knowledge is illusion, we must hold that in thinking we are not reading rationality into an irrational universe but responding to a rationality with which the universe has always been saturated.
—C. S. Lewis, *Christian Reflections*

ACT I: EPIPHANIES BY THE SEA

I was in Australia in the summer of 2004, giving some lectures at the Baptist and Anglican theological colleges on the east coast of that wonderful continent when it hit me. Morling College is in Sydney and the faculty at that institution pride themselves on doing cutting-edge teaching in a postmodern situation, preparing ministers for their largely nonchurchgoing audience. The class to which I had been invited was analyzing films as a tool for ministry. In this particular case, we were analyzing the *Matrix* trilogy, which was filmed in Sydney. There hardly have been more brooding and evocative postmodern works than these three films, synthesizing as they do many ideas and cultural concepts, including Christian ones, into one compelling story about saving humanity from technology run amuck.

I was busily making the point during one session that in a postmodern and largely biblically illiterate culture, the power of one's rhetoric counts far more than the power of one's logic. Persuasion is far more likely to happen by means of powerful and evocative images than by syllogisms. Suddenly, I realized something else as well. While the appeal to the imagination in the postmodern situation time and again trumps the appeal to reason, the church and the academy continue to do theology by and large using an analytical paradigm. Perhaps it is time to ask, "What is wrong with this picture?" Or, better said, "What is wrong with this sort of theologizing that doesn't even involve stories and pictures?"

As I was puzzling over these questions, the thought also dawned on me that we live in an age in which our audiences are primarily and increasingly attuned to visual rather than auditory learning. Hours spent staring at televisions, computer screens, and movies has conditioned us this way. Yet, both in our educational institutions and in our churches we continue to plow the old furrow of worship and classes that primarily amount to an oral delivery of words to listeners. Whereas Jesus' audience well might have responded to the exhortation, "let those who have ears, hear," our audience is more likely to respond to the exhortation, "let those who have eyes, see." Jesus' culture was oral and aural, with only 10 percent or so of the population able to read and write. Our culture, at least nominally, is literate, but frankly prefers seeing to hearing, watching to listening. How many people still listen to baseball games on the radio when they can watch it on television? How many people would rather see a concert than merely hear tunes playing on the radio?

If we are going to do the heavy lifting called hermeneutics in our own cultural situation, it will be good to know with what sort of learners we are dealing and then try to figure out how to reach them. Clearly, simply using more colorful presentations of words and more words projected up on a screen, while helpful, will not be adequate to reach our postmodern world. Something more all-encompassing—appealing to the emotions as well as the mind, to the will as well as the intellect, to the desire to see as well as the need to hear—is required.

Hear the good news: the New Testament writers largely do theology out of a paradigm that appeals to the imagination, including the visual imagination. Therefore, in various ways, it is not that hard to translate such biblical theology into a postmodern situation. As it turns out, premodernity and postmodernity have many things in common—and it is not syllogistic or analytical teaching, preaching, or witnessing. It has far more to do with story, as we shall see.

ACT II: CHANGING THE PARADIGM

Put bluntly, we do not have *theology* in the New Testament. We have what may be called *theologizing*, indeed theologizing into specific cultural settings, whether we are talking about Jesus' parables, Paul's rhetoric, or John's apocalyptic salvos. Traditional Western training has prompted us to think in categories, such as New Testament theology, historical theology, systematic theology, and so on. The fundamental assumption when it comes to the Bible is that the Bible, including the New Testament, is some sort of compendium of theology. Now if one means no more than that, we have plenty of *God-talk* in the Bible (the word *theology* derives from the Greek words *theos* and *logos*). Of course that is true.

What is not true is that the Bible is some sort of manual which synthesizes key ideas and then slots them into categories like eschatology, pneumatology, ecclesiology, theology, Christology, anthropology, and so on. No, that is what scholarly treatment of the Bible has done, seeking to divide its material into isolated concepts that can be analyzed, processed, controlled, and then disseminated. It hardly requires much reflection to realize that this scholarly process involves stripping these ideas of their contexts, particularly their narrative contexts. Perhaps we should have remembered the mantra, "a text without a context is just a pretext for whatever you want it to mean," before we disembodied and disemboweled God-talk from its storied world. There is a further problem too.

The Enlightenment's attempt to treat the Bible in a history-of-ideas kind of way, looking for sources of ideas and then tracing their development (e.g., the concept of Satan is said to come from the intellectual attempt to explain where evil came from if God is all powerful and all good), needs to be seen as an attempt to foist a way of thinking on the text to which the Bible does not very readily submit or yield.

Even before the Enlightenment, the attempt to read the New Testament through the lens of Hellenistic and, particularly, Platonic philosophy led to a skewing of a good deal of the material and a misuse of the data (e.g., the attempt to find an impassable God or to find the Hellenistic notion of the soul in the Bible). The Bible was not written by Hellenistic philosophers, nor was it written by later Christian philosophers, ranging from Augustine to Aquinas to Pascal. It long has been time to change the paradigm when it comes to thinking theologically about the New Testament, and part of this change requires that we recognize the serious flaws in the paradigms we have inherited from nonbiblical sources, both ancient and modern.

The Bible was written entirely, or almost entirely by Jews (the author of Luke and Acts may have been a Gentile, but if so, he was a Gentile who had close contact with the synagogue and knew the Septuagint). Jews told and then wrote down stories; spoke in sapiential ways, using poetry, proverbs, aphorisms, riddles, and parables; and were given to prophetic and apocalyptic oracles. Nothing they wrote reads like a lab manual, philosophical textbook, or scientific treatise. In other words, the sort of speech we find today in the arts rather than in the sciences is far closer to the kind of discourse that early Jews used when they did their God-talk. The good news is that it is this sort of predominantly right-brained discourse that most postmoderns are more attuned to hearing and heeding these days.

I would suggest that the new paradigm for doing theology involves recognizing the following points:

1. Theologizing was done by the biblical writers out of a storied world and into specific situations, using a variety of literary types;

2. The storied world sometimes lies on the surface of the discourse (e.g., in parables), but sometimes it lies beneath the surface and is only alluded to or partially quoted (e.g., in Paul's letters);

3. What we would call concepts or abstract ideas are configured in the storied world, not in some other sort of reasoning.

By this last point I mean, for example, that when Paul thinks of sin, he thinks of the story of Adam; when he thinks of law, he thinks of the story of Moses; when he thinks of faith, he thinks of the story of Abraham; and so on. Even Paul's letters are not compendiums of abstract ideas laid out in syllogisms. The combination of the above points in somewhat reversed order leads to the following paradigm: the symbolic universe of ideas is configured in stories, with the stories then becoming the fodder and framework for theologizing into specific situations. It will be useful at this juncture to give some New Testament core samples of that to which I am referring and then draw some conclusions.

ACT III: JESUS THE SAGE AND STORYTELLER

Everyone seems to love Jesus' parables; unfortunately all too few of us have learned how to properly use them. They are not, and were not, early examples of sermon illustrations. Rather, they were themselves the public preaching tools of Jesus. Like much of sapiential or Wisdom literature, they were intended to be "imagaic," a bit complex, and, whether short or long, they were meant to tease the mind into active thought. Jesus did not believe in the philosophy so often heard today that keeps things at a lowest common denominator, dumbed-down, simple. He believed in appealing to the imagination and teasing even the dullest of minds into active thought. His modus operandi was to boil up the people and engage them in lively discourse, not water down the gospel. He accomplished this by using parables.

Lest we think parables are self-contained, stand-alone units from which we can abstract their historical matrix and use however we please, it needs to be seen that Jesus operated in a specific context where parables were not unusual; people picked up the genre signals and could understand the sort of contextualizing Jesus was doing.

Take, for example, the all-too famous parable of the good Samaritan found in Luke 10. This parable is, in fact, an example of powerful social critique because the antipathy between Jews and Samaritans was considerable in Jesus' day. Samaritans were viewed as half-breeds, heretics, outcasts, and the like; Jews were counseled to avoid them and their country. When they went on pilgrimage to Jerusalem, Jesus' fellow Galileans regularly crossed the Jordan and skirted Samaria so that they would not become ritually unclean on the way to Jerusalem. Jesus, by contrast (see John 4), chose to go right through Samaria and to reach out to Samaritans.

This particular parable gains force when one realizes the following observations:

1. The Samaritan is operating in hostile territory, namely Judea;

2. The lawyer who asked Jesus about neighbors would have identified with the priests and Levites, for whom experts in the law regularly worked;

3. The priest and Levite probably would have seen the man left for dead on the side of the road as potentially a source of

uncleanness—contracting corporal uncleanness would have meant they couldn't go to work for a week. By passing by on the other side of the road, they are thus likely being portrayed in a self-serving mode; and

4. The man lying on the side of the road was surely a Jew, and so it was not the Samaritan, but the priest and the Levite, who primarily had a duty of neighborliness to him.

In addition, we may note that Jesus really skewers the lawyer by telling him to go act like the Samaritan. Jesus was seeking to break down social barriers as part of the divine saving activity known as the Kingdom or Dominion of God that Jesus was inaugurating. He refused to address the limiting question, "Who is my neighbor?" that has as its subtext, "Who do I not need to treat as neighbor?" Instead, he provided an example of how we are to be neighbors to one and all. Note that the phrase good Samaritan, unlike the way we use the phrase today, would have been seen as an oxymoron in first-century Judea.

What we should learn from the above observations is that even though these parables are somewhat self-contained stories, they cannot be used properly without understanding their original context. The context of origin must be allowed to condition how we read and thus use and contextualize these parables today. In other words, in our biblically illiterate culture, we must ourselves do homework to make sure we are not misusing these stories. They were never intended as tools to teach general ethical maxims. They are stories about what happens when God's saving activity breaks into our midst.

Another example from the parables of Jesus further clarifies that context and history are important elements in properly understanding Scripture. Consider now the parable of the sower found in Mark 4, where the sower sows the seed that falls on different kinds of soil. The fruitfulness of the plant that grows from the seed is, in large part, dependent on the condition of the soil in which the seed is planted. This popular parable has sometimes come under scholarly suspicion because it seems too much like a Christian allegory. The different soils represent different people and their levels of receptivity to the gospel, and the sower is obviously Jesus or Jesus' disciples, with the seed being the Word. The truth is, however, that ancient Jewish parables frequently had allegorical elements in them. They did not necessarily seek to make only one point. Indeed, they might make several points, though all of Jesus' parables are about the dawning Dominion of God.

To understand Mark 4, several things need to be borne in mind. Parables were not intended to be literal descriptions of first-century practices. They were often lifelike, but not literal transcripts of reality. Indeed, it is often the case in Jesus' parables that one can tell when Jesus is making a kingdom point when the story veers off from reality into hyperbole. The yields of grain spoken of at the end of this parable are in fact astronomical. The point is not verisimilitude, but rather that Kingdom work, despite many failures, can yield successes out of all proportion to the work done on producing the crop. In other words, the outcome has to do with God's lavish grace, not merely human effort. What is especially interesting and telling about this story is that, if indeed it is a comment by Jesus on his own ministry, it speaks not only of many failures but also of some outstanding successes. The Word often fell either on deaf ears, into the lives of distracted persons, or into the lives of persons only partially willing to allow the Kingdom message to take root within them.

At the same time, Jesus does realistically speak of certain kinds of agricultural practices of his day—we must think of a tenant farmer who is trying so desperately to produce a crop that every inch of soil is being used, whatever its caliber or character. The Word should be prolifically spread abroad, without picking in advance a target audience. Notice that what makes the difference between acceptance and rejection of the Word is the soil it lodges in. The sower, the Word, and the nurture of sun and rain are the same in all cases. It is the difference in the soil that makes the difference in receptivity. This is hardly a predestinarian parable. The soil decides the issue, not the sower.

What do we learn from these wonderful stories? We learn that context matters. We also learn that there is a complexity rather than opacity to these stories. They have a variety of points, and they require of us a variety of sensitivities if we are to understand them and properly apply the truths they convey.

Finally, it is not enough to tell or retell the story. Notice at the end of both of these parables how Jesus seeks to apply or explain them. Telling the story is not enough. Placing one's audience within the story requires more than that. In regard to the one who wishes to sow these parables today, a detailed knowledge of both the ancient and modern horizons or contexts is needed.

ACT IV: PAUL THE RHETORICIAN AND HIS STORIED WORLD

We have already alluded to the fact that Paul thinks out of biblical stories and into his church situations. The failure to recognize this truth has led to all sorts of misinterpretations of Paul's letters, including Romans, the most used and abused of all those letters. My concern here is to point out that this letter is a word on target for Paul's audience in Rome in the late 50s A.D. and is not a compendium of Paul's greatest theological and ethical hits. Notice that such important Pauline topics as resurrection or the Lord's Supper hardly come up for discussion in Romans. Romans must not be seen as an introduction to Pauline theology. Paul's rhetoric and storied world affects what he is saying and we need to know those things if we are to make sense of his discourse.

Consider the comparison of the first and last Adams in Romans 5:12-21. Here, Paul's storied world comes to the surface of the discourse. As we have already pointed out, when Paul thinks about sin, he thinks of the story of Adam. He does not think of sin in an abstract way, but rather in a personal way, especially when the issue is from where sin came. In this lively comparison and contrast between Jesus and Adam, Paul assumes that both are progenitors of a whole race of people; as progenitors they affect all those who are "in" them. In Paul's storied world, you are either in Adam or in Christ, but you can't be in both at once.

It is in part because of the failure to pick up the narrative signals that there has been so much confusion when it comes to interpreting Romans 7:7-13 and 7:14-25. Part of the confusion has been caused by failing to realize that the story of Adam and Christ is still in play and presupposed in Romans 7. The rest of the confusion comes from lack of recognition of the rhetorical signals. Paul is using here the rhetorical device known as speech in character (prosopopoeia) in this chapter.

Put succinctly, Romans 7:7-13 is the story of Adam retold, and Romans 7:14-25 is the story of all those who are "in Adam" and outside of Christ. In other words, Christian psychologists need to stop reading Romans 7 as if it were a transcript telling us about the psychological dilemmas of Christians caught between a rock and a hard place. On the contrary, here we have a discussion of those lost in the bondage of sin and outside of Christ. If one wants to hear the story about the tensions in the Christian life and the issue of sin for the Christian, one must look elsewhere

(Galatians 5, for example). In Romans 7 the use of "I" is a typical rhetorical device to make the story come to life and make vivid the points Paul is making—the "I" is not Paul, but Adam in the first passage, and those "in Adam" in 7:14-25.

There are several contextual factors that are crucial for understanding Romans 7. Romans 7:4-5 and Romans 8:1-2 clearly say that Christians are no longer in the flesh, no longer subject to the bondage of the rule of sin and death in their lives. On the contrary, they have been set free by the Spirit ruling in their lives. Believers are dead to that which once held them captive. Notice how the "I" in Romans 7:7-13 was once alive apart from and before the law. In Paul's storied world, this state describes only one person—Adam. Only he existed before any law or commandment was given. Also, 7:7-13 only speaks of one commandment to which this person is beholden. Again, this describes only Adam, the man who was given but one commandment.

There is, then, a clear connection here between sin and death, in the same way we heard of it in Romans 5:12-21. Notice the total absence of reference to the Holy Spirit in both Romans 7:7-13 and 14-25. This "I," unlike Paul and other Christians, does not have the Holy Spirit in his life; he can only cry out, "Who will deliver me from this body of death?" Romans 7:14-25 follows from Romans 2–3 where Paul told us that even Gentiles had the law of God in some fashion written on their hearts or minds. Thus, 7:14-25 need not be specifically about Jews who have the law in their minds; this passage could be about Jews or Gentiles or both, but in any case it is those who are outside of Christ. Thinking narratively about Romans 7–8 and noticing the progression of the discourse, it is logical to conclude that in Romans 7:14-25 we have a vivid description of someone outside of Christ but, at the point of conviction and conversion, crying out for deliverance. This person realizes that he must do better, knows something of what God requires, but is unable to do it. Romans 7:25a and Romans 8:1-17 provide the panacea and the answer for the lost person: it can be found in Jesus Christ. Unfortunately, we often read this narrative anachronistically because we have been influenced by Christian theologians throughout history who were often influenced by the historical situation in which they found themselves. That led to a distortion in our understanding of whom Paul is describing. For example, Augustine was writing in the fourth century as the Roman Empire was disintegrating. Luther was writing in the sixteenth century as nation-states were coming into power and the church was in a period of widespread corruption.

Herein lies a further lesson. It is not enough to read the text "narrato-logically"—it all depends on whose story you are reading into this text. The answer needs to be plausible in terms of the storied world of Paul. Texts such as Philippians 3:6 make perfectly clear that Romans 7 cannot be said to be a personal transcript of Paul's own Jewish or Christian experience. No, Paul is speaking more generically of all those who are in Adam and outside of Christ, crying out for redemption. We must not merely recognize a story but recognize whose story it is before we start preaching and teaching texts like this one.

ACT V: THE APOCALYPTIC IMAGINATION OF JOHN

In this essay I have deliberately chosen three very different sorts of texts reflecting three different genre of literature: parable, rhetorical dis-course in a letter, and, now, apocalyptic prophecy. I have chosen three different genres to help make the point that story is fundamental and undergirds them all. Story is the constant in the theologizing of these dif-ferent New Testament figures. Here I must turn to the Apocalypse to give one further example.

It is true that most readers of Revelation, at least intuitively, realize that this material, while it must be taken seriously, nevertheless can't be taken literally. John is not really envisioning multiheaded beasts roaming the earth. Such images are ciphers and symbols for all-too-human and, in other cases, divine beings. Yet even this portion of Scripture sometimes has been read literally.

Back in the late 1960s, I was riding down the Blue Ridge Parkway in the mountains of North Carolina when the clutch of my father's '55 Chevy blew out. My friend Doug and I had to coast down an exit ramp and limp into a gas station. The mechanic there did not have the right parts or knowledge to fix the car, so we found ourselves hitchhiking back to the middle of the state. We were picked up by a very elderly couple in an old Plymouth. It turns out they were "flat-landers." When this fact came to light, my friend began to argue and ask why they thought the world was flat. The answer was given, "It says in the book of Revelations that the angels will stand on the four corners of the earth. The earth can't be round if it has four corners." Beware of those who begin sentences with, "It says in the book of Revelations (plural) . . ."

The problem, of course, was that this couple assumed that Revelation was indeed seeking to teach cosmology, rather than merely suggesting that the angels would cover and come from all points on the compass. This couple took the book of Revelation seriously and referentially, but they mistook figuratively referential speech for literally referential speech. They had made a genre mistake—not an uncommon mistake when it comes to Revelation.

What is interesting about Revelation is that while it alludes to all kinds of stories both biblical and extra-biblical (including ancient combat myths), it seldom quotes the Old Testament. It has more echoes and allusions to the Old Testament than any other book, yet has almost no quotes from there. What are we to make of this fact?

The author of Revelation assumes the audience already knows the stories of Adam, Elijah, Moses, the Exodus, and many others. Thus, the author feels free to draw on them tangentially and to reconfigure them in his telling of what "was, and is, and is to come." He focuses the story in light of both the Christ story and the story of his converts, partially retold in Revelation 2–3. Story functions in Revelation as subtext and text, being both behind and part of the ongoing narrative told in Revelation 6–22. This brings up the very good point that the New Testament writers and speakers all tend to reconfigure their Old Testament stories in light of more recent developments, in particular, developments that involve Jesus and the dominion. Even more interesting is that apocalyptic prophecy becomes the vehicle allowing for the telling of the future story of God's people. John doesn't just serve up elliptical oracles about the future, he serves up oracles that tell a tale about the future.

What is also seldom realized about apocalyptic prophecy is that it is often deliberately multivalent; for example, Mr. 666 is Nero, Domitian, or any other megalomaniac ruler lusting after worship and world domination. The beast in the author's context was the Roman Empire, but it could be any evil empire. When it comes to the future, God reveals enough about its character so that we may have hope, but not so much about its details that we no longer feel the need to exercise faith.

Just because these prophecies are referential does not mean you are meant to pin them down to one set of referents. That's hardly how apocalyptic writing works. It deliberately uses generic and universal symbols when speaking of the future. It is crucial, then, neither to dismiss these stories as fractured fairy tales nor to try and pin them down to one late twentieth or early twenty-first century set of referents. Indeed, I would stress that John was speaking in the first instance to his own century and people, who certainly had no knowledge or interest in figures that would arise two thousand years later. No, Revelation is a word on target for the seven churches precisely because the battle between good and evil transpires in every generation and often takes similar forms along the way. The devil, as it turns out, is not very original and creative, so he keeps playing out his tale and spinning his stories the same way over and over again.

To make our point clearer, consider for a minute Revelation 12. The woman clothed with the sun can be seen to be both Mother Zion (i.e., the Old Testament people of God configured as a woman) and Mother Mary who gives birth to a male child destined to rule the nations. Satan seeks unsuccessfully to destroy the mother and child—indeed, so unsuccessfully that the child ends up sitting on a throne in heaven, and Satan ends up cast out of that self-same heavenly realm. Unable to destroy the child-prodigy-savior figure, he turns his wrath on the woman who flees into the wilderness. While Satan seeks to flood her out, she is protected there in the wilderness. This wilderness certainly is not an image of heaven, but rather an image of a lost earth no longer in harmony with its original creation design. The theology of rapture is not for John. The people of God will be protected from Satan's wrath on earth, not by escaping to heaven. Unable to destroy the woman even while she is on earth, Satan turns his attention to her children.

Here is both a cautionary tale meant to warn the converts in Asia that they are under attack from the powers of darkness and a hopeful tale promising that God will not allow the gates of Hades to prevail against the church—it will endure and prevail. While this is a Christian story, it is a story that draws on both Old Testament imagery (the rainbow from the Noah story) and ancient combat myths (here the angel Michael does battle with Satan and casts him to earth).

A word of caution to interpreters of Revelation: if you don't know and understand the underlying stories here, you will misread the plot and the way John uses these stories. In other words, doing theology in a narratological way does not give us permission to ignore the historical contexts of our New Testament stories—even in a postmodern setting. There are both good and bad ways to retell these New Testament stories and, in this regard, good and bad theologizing happens when we do so. Even though it is story, it is important to get the story right.

ACT VI: AND SO?

This essay has been a short odyssey through the storied world of the New Testament, helping us to rethink what we mean by theology and theologizing. I am saying theology and theologizing have everything to do with story and storytelling. We need to get beyond both ancient and modern ways of handling the text that strip away the story, leaving a mass of quivering ideas and concepts that we then are free to rearrange in any order that pleases us. Such stripping and rearranging may be an intellectually satisfying exercise for some, but it turns out to be a way of neutralizing the story and not allowing it to have its intended effect on us. That method of interpretation is an attempt to take control over these stories before they fully take hold of us. If that is what thinking theologically and doing theology amounts to, then we need a moratorium on thinking and doing theology.

I would call us, however, not to a sabbatical from theology but to do our theologizing in the very same manner as Jesus and the biblical authors. That is, by using story, and especially the story of Jesus. I would offer the encouragement that our postmodern situation gives us a new opportunity to re-present the story in vividly new ways.

Whatever we may have thought about the flaws in Mel Gibson's movie, *The Passion of the Christ,* it is a compelling presentation. The emotional power of its dramatization of the story carried the day for many in the audience, leaving some numb and others deeply moved. My point is simply that in the postmodern age where visual symbol, sign, story, and narrative are poignant, we would be foolish not to use them to tell and retell the old, old story. In fact, Jesus and his followers will rise up and call us blessed if we do so, for by creatively retelling the story as a way of doing theology, we will be following in the sacred footsteps of our inspired forebears.

THE ESSENCE OF THE GOSPEL

Maxie D. Dunnam

The true acceptance of the word requires that we do not let it lie only on the surface of our minds, nor be satisfied only to have it penetrate a little deeper and take root in our emotions, or let competing desires grow up unchecked. Instead, we must cherish the word of truth in our deepest hearts, guard it against foes, let it rule there, and mold our conduct to its principles.
—Alexander Maclaren,
Expositions of Holy Scripture

Therefore, since through God's mercy we have this ministry, we do not lose heart. Rather, we have renounced secret and shameful ways; we do not use deception, nor do we distort the word of God. On the contrary, by setting forth the truth plainly we commend ourselves to every man's conscience in the sight of God. And even if our gospel is veiled, it is veiled to those who are perishing. The god of this age has blinded the minds of unbelievers, so that they cannot see the light of the gospel of the glory of Christ, who is the image of God. For we do not preach ourselves, but Jesus Christ as Lord, and ourselves as your servants for Jesus' sake. For God, who said, "Let light shine out of darkness," made his light shine in our hearts to give us the light of the knowledge of the glory of God in the face of Christ. (2 Corinthians 4:1-6 NIV)

I don't know how it is with you, but I can recall occasions when a text of Scripture grabbed my imagination, gripped my mind, burrowed its way into my soul, and became part of my being. In many instances, I can relive the setting when those things happened, and they energize me. The passage of 2 Corinthians 4:1-6 is such a case. It was senior recognition day at Candler School of Theology at Emory University in 1958. I was graduating. The dean had invited Dow Kirkpatrick to speak for our senior recognition service. Dow was at his best—and that was great.

He told a story I think I shall never forget. It came out of the World Methodist Conference that had met in Oxford in 1951. The high point of that program was the service held in St. Mary's Church (the university church) commemorating John and Charles Wesley. There was only one man alive at that time who was the right man to preach on such an occasion. He was John Scott Lidgett, then over ninety years old. Lidgett remembered hearing his grandmother tell her memories of having heard John Wesley preach.

Lidgett was in good health, but didn't have much strength. His doctors decided that if they could conserve his strength, he might be able to preach that evening. He was brought to Oxford on the train and put in a hotel to rest. Then he was dressed in his preaching robe and brought to the church in an automobile. The pulpit chair was carried out to the car; he was put in it and then carried up to the platform. He didn't stand during the service until the time to preach. He preached almost thirty minutes—vigorously. Then, just as he initiated the closing prayer, he swooned—every ounce of energy having gone from him. Many in the congregation undoubtedly thought they were witnessing the passing of a great man. Lidgett was taken from the church and then taken in an ambulance back to his hotel room where a doctor was waiting. The report is that at about two o'clock in the morning, he roused, opened his eyes, and said, "Preaching always did take something out of me."

Well, it does, and it should. My calling to preach was confirmed on that senior recognition day at Candler School of Theology about fifty years ago. For me that day was one of those "Mount Tabor experiences" we can never quite forget—when God allows us to see an extra portion of the glory, and in the ecstasy of that experience lays God's claim upon our lives.

I'm sure I had read that Scripture before then, but it had not made an impact upon me. That day it did. It penetrated to the deepest core of my being, enveloped my soul, and has been a part of me ever since. Hear the last verse again: "For God, who said, 'Let light shine out of darkness,' made his light shine in our hearts to give us the light of the knowledge of the glory of God in the face of Christ" (2 Corinthians 4:6 NIV). I don't know another text that gathers up the essence of the gospel as that one does. I mean by "essence" what the dictionaries say: the distinctive quality that constitutes what something is.

Now, that which makes the gospel what it is, is in that Scripture and there's only one word for it: *incredible.* The radiant glory of God shines in the face of Jesus—this statement is the incredibility of the Incarnation. The radiant glory of God shining in the face of Jesus Christ has shined in our hearts—this fact is the incredibility of the Christian experience. The radiant glory of God shining in the face of Jesus Christ that has shined in our hearts is ours to declare—this message is the incredibility of the Christian witness.

That's the way the text breaks itself down, which is the essence of the gospel. So, let us look at the message through the Incarnation, Christian experience, and Christian witness. All of these things together are the essence of the gospel.

INCARNATION

First we consider the Incarnation. This is Christianity's unique claim. The radiant glory of God shines in the face of Jesus Christ. This is incredible—God's ultimate revelation is Jesus Christ. The Church has labeled this fact the Incarnation.

Let me suggest a contrast. There were few people in the twentieth century who seemed as immortal as Mao Tse-Tung. Chairman Mao became the incarnation of a movement, a system of thought, and a revolution that impacted nine hundred million people. He lived to be eighty-three years old and was China's leader for over three decades. Even the most astute observer found it difficult to imagine a China without Chairman Mao. Yet he died. An admirer, Orville Schell, wrote shortly after Mao's death that, "He conceived of the Chinese revolution, and then helped cause it to happen, and in the process, every thought of Chairman Mao became the primary thought of almost every Chinese. The word almost literally became flesh."[1]

Note the conditional word *almost*—"the word almost became flesh." The Gospel of John says of Jesus, "The Word became flesh" (John 1:14

NIV). There is no reservation or conditional definition. And Paul wrote the Corinthians, "God . . . made his light shine in our hearts to give us the light of the knowledge of the glory of God in the face of Christ" (2 Corinthians 4:6 NIV).

I was in China two years after Mao's death. His likeness in picture and statue was still everywhere. The little red book of quotations was still in all the bookstores. Chairman Mao will take his place in history with other great shapers of national life. A limitation is still there, however. When I was in China in 1979, the magnificent mausoleum that had been built for Mao was closed. The official word was that it was closed for repairs, but the informal word passed on among the guides was that the closing was a deliberate effort to diminish Mao's presence in the minds and hearts of the people. That diminishing effort continues in China today.

In Mao—powerful man that he was—the word *almost* became flesh. With Jesus, the Word *did* become flesh and dwelt among us. Jesus is central in the gospel because Jesus is God's movement of love toward us. Jesus is God's invitation to salvation and eternal life. Jesus is God's affirmation that we are not left to make it on our own. We're not forgotten, we're not forsaken, and we're not given up to be strangers and sojourners in a foreign land with no signals or no destination to direct us. Jesus is God's "Yes" to life after death and our eternal salvation.

Some time ago, a group of historians gathered and, for fun, decided to rewrite history as if certain things had not happened. What would history be like if Napoleon had come to America, if the Moors had won the war in Spain, if Booth had missed Lincoln, if Lee had won at Gettysburg. The biggest "if" of all history they did not contemplate was what if God had not sent the Son.

A pastor I know preached a powerful sermon using the rubric "If God Had Stayed at Home"—if God had not come to us in Jesus Christ. If God had stayed home, we would not know who God is and what God is like. If God had stayed at home, there would be no salvation, no answer to our sins. If God had stayed at home, we would not have power over Satan. If God had stayed at home, there would be no victory over death, no promise and certainty of life eternal.

But God didn't stay at home. God walked down the stairway of heaven holding a little baby—the Incarnation and the Word became flesh. God has become one with us to make us one with God. If we don't get this fact in our understanding of the gospel, we don't get the rest of the story. If we don't begin here, there's no place to go. There will be no renewal of the church, no revival of faith among us, and no witnessing to the world unless we lodge this truth solidly in our minds and hearts and proclaim it unreservedly. The radiant glory of God shines in the face of Jesus Christ. That's the incredibility of the Incarnation.

CHRISTIAN EXPERIENCE

A second ingredient in the essence of the gospel is the Christian experience. The radiant glory of God shining in the face of Jesus Christ has shined in our hearts, said Paul. This fact is salvation; this is conversion. That's what it means to be a Christian. I believe in being born again. I believe in this phenomenon because Jesus calls us to it. I also believe in this because I've experienced it. Even so, though I believe in being born again, I pray that the day will soon come when we won't have to talk about being born-again Christians. For that phrase is redundant. If one is a Christian, then one is born again. If one is born again, then one is a Christian. We are talking about a life-or-death issue, a choice between eternal life or eternal death. How this happens is not the issue, but that it happens is the most important thing in the world. There is no Christian tradition without some personal encounter with the living Christ.

I heard a story about a spouse who was berating the partner for extravagant spending. "How many times do I have to tell you," the spouse warned angrily, "that it's economically unsound to spend money before you get it?" That didn't intimidate the other spouse one bit. "Oh, I don't know about that," was the reply. "This way, if you don't get the money, at least you have something to show for it."

If you have had a Christian experience—whether you talk about it in terms of being born again, a new life in Christ, or the light of the knowledge of God shining in the face of Jesus Christ—then it doesn't matter how you talk about it, for you have something to show for it.

Let me illustrate with a story. I'll call her Judy. She was no more than twenty-five when I met her. A lot of living—too much of the wrong kind of living—had been packed into those twenty-five years. Two marriages (the first ending in divorce, the second ending with her husband's suicide), two stints in mental hospitals, and enslavement to alcohol and drugs were all part of her lightless life.

Judy called what occurred in her life a miracle, and I don't know a better word for it. A friend whom she had met at work believed that the power of the gospel is relevant to our day, that Christ can and will transform anyone who will repent, accept him as Savior, and give themselves to his lordship. This friend shared that gospel with Judy, loved Judy, prayed for and with Judy, until one day these things happened. Judy repented, accepted the forgiveness of Christ, took that beautiful step of faith, received Christ, and surrendered herself to his lordship. Change began to take place, not everything and not all at once, but a dramatic transformation began. When Judy shared her whole story with me, she had not had a drink in eight months. She was off drugs and her periods of depression were getting farther apart. She was still nervous and talked jerkily. The marks of her sojourn in the far country were still upon her. But as she talked, I knew, in the words of Paul, that the light of the knowledge of the glory of God was *shining on her face*.

I share this dramatic story to make the point that if Christ can save to the uttermost as he did with Judy, he can save any of us. We may not be in prisons or have any destructive addictions, but he can and wants to heal our wounded psyches. Judy responded and opened her life to Christ's healing promise. The last time Judy spoke with me, a new calmness was present. She affirmed a quality of inner peace that had never been in her life and which she could not manufacture on her own. This is the Christian experience.

A second story further illustrates this point. A young man I'll call Larry, about thirty-five to forty years old, asked to see me. He shared the sad news that he was having to leave our church because his job was taking him to another city. He was very sad because he didn't want to leave this church. Yet, there was a radiant joy about him as he reminded me of the commitment to Christ that he had made in our church about a year earlier. His was not a dramatic experience. He was not delivered from drugs or alcohol or from a sordid past. Even so, he needed the light of the knowledge of the glory of God. Larry's was a quiet but definite experience in which he came to the conviction that something was missing in his life. Before he was touched by the Christian experience, he was without spiritual direction and meaning. There was no assurance of salvation. There was no joy in his life. Then, his newfound commitment led him to tithe his income, a discipline that he said was giving him incomparable joy. He also had come to live daily with Scripture, a practice enriching his life by deepening and informing his faith. His faith also put him to praying, and now prayer had become a vital reality to him as he talked and listened to God. As Larry spoke to me, I know I didn't imagine that the radiant glory of God shining in the face of Jesus Christ was also *shining in his face*. That's the Christian experience.

I share these two stories to make the point that the Christian experience is needed by all of us. There may be no glaring sins in our lives. We may not be imprisoned by destructive habits. We may simply have a gnawing restlessness that keeps us moving hither and yon, jumping from one effort to another to find meaning. We may simply have the vague but painful stirrings within us that don't go away when we get that new car or new job or new house that we thought would make us happy. We may simply feel an aching void because we haven't confessed our sins to another person because everybody thinks we have it made, and we don't think they would understand. Wherever we are in life, the radiant glory of God shining in the face of Jesus Christ shines in our hearts. And that's what the gospel is all about.

More than conversion, though, the Christian experience is what Paul called a life in Christ. Listen to Paul writing to the Colossians:

> Now I rejoice in what was suffered for you, and I fill up in my flesh what is still lacking in regard to Christ's afflictions, for the sake of his body, which is the church. I have become its servant by the commission God gave me to present to you the word of God in its fullness—the mystery that has been kept hidden for ages and generations, but is now disclosed to the saints. To them God has chosen to make known among the Gentiles the glorious riches of this mystery, which is Christ in you, the hope of glory. (Colossians 1:24-27 NIV)

Paul's great definition of a Christian was a person in Christ. Paul used the picture of "in Christ" over and over again. That phrase or its equivalent is used at least 172 times in Paul's epistles. His most vivid description of his own life was written to the Galatians: "I have been crucified with Christ and I no longer live, but Christ lives in me. The life I live in the body, I live by faith in the Son of God, who loved me and gave himself for me" (Galatians 2:20 NIV).

In one of the boldest prayers ever prayed, Paul interceded for the Ephesians. If you believe Scripture as I do, he also interceded for us:

> I pray that from his glorious, unlimited resources he will give you mighty inner strength through his Holy Spirit. And I pray that Christ will be

more and more at home in your hearts as you trust in him. May your roots go down deep into the soil of God's marvelous love. And may you have the power to understand, as all God's people should, how wide, how long, how high, and how deep his love really is. May you experience the love of Christ, though it is so great you will never fully understand it. Then you will be filled with the fullness of life and power that comes from God. (Ephesians 3:16–19 NLT)

This is quite a revelation that you and I may attain the fullness of life and power from God, the fullness of being, the fullness of God himself.

One of my most vivid memories to which I return often in my mind was an evening I spent with a friend, a Trappist monk named Brother Sam. While the ways he and I lived out our lives were vastly different, we felt a real kinship and oneness of spirit together. One evening he and I were alone and were sharing our Christian journeys with each other. The highlight of that evening was his relating to me the occasion of his solemn vows, the service when he made his life commitment to the monastic community and way of life.

On that occasion, he prostrated himself before the altar of the chapel in the very spot where his coffin will be set when he dies. As he lay covered in a funeral pall, the death bell that tolls at the earthly parting of a brother sounded the solemn gongs of death. Then there was silence, the silence of death. The silence of the gathered community was broken by the words of "For you have died, and your life is hidden with Christ in God" (Colossians 3:3 NAB). After that powerful word, there was more silence as Brother Sam meditated on his solemn vow. Then the community broke into song with the words of Psalm 118, which is sometimes a part of the Easter service in Catholic liturgies, "I shall not die but live/ and declare the deeds of the LORD" (Psalm 118:17 NAB).

After this resurrection proclamation, the deacon shouted the words from Ephesians, "Awake, O sleeper, / and arise from the dead, / and Christ will give you light" (Ephesians 5:14 NAB). Then the loud bells of the abbey rang joyfully. Brother Sam rose, the funeral pall fell off, and the robe of the monastic order was placed on him. He received the kiss of peace and was welcomed into the community to live a life hid in Christ.

We share in this mystery. Almost every day for the past thirty years, my morning ritual has included a word to myself. Sometimes I speak it aloud, sometimes I simply register it in my awareness, sometimes I make it a litany to a breathing-in and breathing-out exercise. The word is this: "Maxie, the secret is simply this: Christ in you! Yes, Christ in you bringing with him the hope of all glorious things to come." That is J. B. Phillips's translation of Colossians 1:27 addressed to me personally. If there is one thing that has kept me going and growing for nearly thirty years now, it is the truth that at a crucial point in my life I turned to God's Word to give perspective and direction to my frazzled life. This was God's gift to me.

I believe it is this understanding of the indwelling Christ that gives both definition and power to our holiness. Holiness is not something we achieve; like salvation, it is a gift. Holiness is not just a one-time gift, even for the persons who experience a second work of grace. It is not a finished work. The work is ongoing as we abide in Christ and daily yield ourselves to His perfecting power.

We do well to always remember the metaphor Jesus used when he called us to abide in him. The marvelous fifteenth chapter of John's Gospel begins with the illuminating metaphor of the vines and the branches. Jesus tells who he is in relation to the Father and tells who God the Father is in relation to him. Then Jesus tells who we are in relation to himself.

> I am the true vine, and my Father is the gardener. He cuts off every branch in me that bears no fruit, while every branch that does bear fruit he prunes so that it will be even more fruitful. You are already clean because of the word I have spoken to you. Remain in me, and I will remain in you. No branch can bear fruit by itself; it must remain in the vine. Neither can you bear fruit unless you remain in me. I am the vine; you are the branches. If a man remains in me and I in him, he will bear much fruit; apart from me you can do nothing. If anyone does not remain in me, he is like a branch that is thrown away and withers; such branches are picked up, thrown into the fire and burned. If you remain in me and my words remain in you, ask whatever you wish, and it will be given you. (John 15:1-7 NIV)

This is an extravagant promise that if we will abide in him, he will abide in us. Isn't this the definition and the power for holiness? Isn't this the core of the Christian experience?

CHRISTIAN WITNESS

There is even more in the text of 2 Corinthians 4. The light of the knowledge of the glory of God shines in the face of Jesus Christ—that is the incredibility of the Incarnation. The light of the knowledge of the glory of God shining in the face of Jesus Christ has shined in our hearts—that is the incredibility of the Christian experience. Add to these that the light of the knowledge of the glory of God shining in the face of Jesus Christ that has shone in our hearts is ours to declare—that is the incredibility of the Christian witness. Witness is the vocation of every Christian. This vocation is connected with, defined through, and empowered by the facts of the Incarnation and the Christian experience that we have been exploring.

Let me put these thoughts into three clear and dogmatic assertions. What we think of Jesus Christ will determine what we do about evangelism. If we can at least begin to comprehend that Jesus Christ is not only the Second Person of the Trinity, but that he is also the human embodiment of God, then we can begin to comprehend what a relationship with Jesus could mean for people and the awesome spectrum of Jesus' work and ministry. Therefore, Paul was always sounding the note of Incarnation in such powerful assertions as that "In Christ God was reconciling the world to himself" (2 Corinthians 5:19).

What we think about grace shapes our evangelistic message. What we think about grace determines our evangelistic urgency. John Wesley did us a great service by providing a distinctive emphasis when talking about grace in three specific ways: prevenient grace, justifying grace, and sanctifying grace. Prevenient grace is the grace of God going before us, pulling us, wooing us, seeking to open our minds and hearts, and eventually giving us faith. Justifying grace is God's forgiving love freely given to us, reconciling us, putting us right with God, making Christ who knew no sin to be sin on our behalf. Sanctifying grace is the work and spirit of Christ within us restoring the broken image, completing the salvation that was begun in justification, and bringing us to complete newness of life as we are perfected in love.

Certainly our understanding and experience of grace impacts our witness and determines in large part the way we do evangelism. If we believe that God loves us and all people, seeking people before they seek God, then we witness with confidence and humility. We know that we cannot limit the saving love of God and know that we do not do the saving work but rather God does.

All of this leads to the third assertion: What we think Jesus can do for a person will determine what we will do about evangelism and mission. The uniqueness of Jesus Christ as God's complete gift of himself for our salvation and sanctification is being challenged in our day. I remember a word that came out of the evangelism section of the World Council of Churches that met several years ago. They were talking about universal salvation (and the notion that Jesus is not the only way to salvation) when a bishop from Pakistan got up and said to the group, "If what you say is true—that Jesus is not the unique Savior of the world, God's only gift of salvation—then I will go home and tell my people they do not have to die anymore." He makes the point in a very stark yet profound way. Our understanding of who Jesus was and is and why he came into the world will determine our understanding of witness to his life and mission in the world and will shape the urgency with which we work.

Do you believe that humankind is lost? Do you believe Peter when he says, "There is salvation in no one else, for there is no other name under heaven given among mortals by which we must be saved" (Acts 4:12). Do you believe that Jesus Christ can reconcile relationships, heal diseases, cast out demons, give direction and meaning, and sustain us in hope when the world is crumbling around us? What we believe Jesus Christ can do for persons will determine what we do for evangelism. The vocation of every Christian is witness. Remember, *there may be someone in whom the light of the glory of God will never shine unless it shines through you.*

THE FULLNESS OF LEARNING
Paul W. Chilcote

*The refinement or crudity of theological and philosophical
thinking is itself, of course, one of the measures of the state
of our culture; and the tendency in some quarters to reduce
theology to such principles as a child can understand or a
Socinian accept, is itself indicative of cultural debility.*
—T. S. Eliot, *Notes Towards the Definition of Culture*

Theological education is a formational process. All education that
is worthwhile involves transformation. I suppose I had known
these things intuitively from an early age, but nothing secured
these commitments in my own teaching more than my encounter with
the idea of "training for transformation" in Africa. In their three-volume
handbook of this title, Anne Hope and Sally Timmel state on the opening page that, "Development, liberation and transformation are all
aspects of the same process. It is not a marginal activity. It is at the core
of all creative human living."[1]

While this vision of education is ancient, Paulo Freire, in his landmark
study *Pedagogy of the Oppressed*, resurrected the simple idea that learning
is not about the passive reception of information but is meant to awaken
and develop the ability for creative intelligence. At the core of his
concept of transformative education is the theory of dialogical action.[2] To

put it all rather simply, education is meant to be a process of liberation "from the inside out," not an external and authoritarian imposition of ideas or values that can easily misshape the human spirit. Theological education, using this paradigm, is a process of self-discovery, liberation, and formation from the inside out; it is a process that permits the Spirit of God to transform men and women so they may discover their true identity as the children of God.

The ancient Greeks employed a concept that comes very close to this formational vision, namely *paideia*.[3] The term can be translated in a number of different ways—as instruction, nurture, education, training, guidance, even chastisement—but its primary meaning is life-shaping discipline. *Paideia* is essentially instruction through action. Related very closely to character formation, it involves a lifelong process of learning and growth. It implies a journey. Werner Jaeger, in his monumental three-volume study of this concept, shows that the idea represented to the ancient Greeks an enormous ideological task.[4] They were concerned with nothing less than the fundamental shaping of the ideal human being.

Paul draws upon this classical idea and places the concept of formation at the center of his admonition to Christian parents in Ephesians 6:4. He commands parents to bring up their children "in the discipline and instruction of the Lord." For the early Christian, this theological education must have meant something like the use of action directed toward the moral and spiritual nurture and training of the followers of Jesus. It entailed all of those things done in the community of faith that shape the whole person in the journey toward maturity in Christ. That is a big idea, a goal referred to rather explicitly by the writer to the Hebrews: "We had human parents to discipline us, and we respected them . . . But [God] disciplines us for our good, in order that we may share his holiness" (Hebrews 12:9-10). This form of discipline is nothing less than seeking wisdom in community.

In the English language, the words "discipline" and "disciple" obviously come from the same root. A disciple is simply a learner. A disciple of Christ is a person who has consented to place him or herself under the *paideia* of the Lord, the true purpose of which is liberation. Unless you discipline yourself in practice in an effort to learn how to play the piano, for example, you will never be free to release the music that is in your soul. This is a vision well worth our rediscovery in relation to theological education today. Moreover, it resonates well, I believe, with the Wesleyan heritage in which I stand.

In this brief essay, therefore, I want to explore theological education as *paideia*. In the context of the Christian seminary—and particularly for one that stands in the Wesleyan tradition—this process will entail all of those actions within a vital community of faith that shape men and women in the journey toward maturity in Christian calling and leadership. Several of the constitutive aspects of *paideia* in this context include commitment, community, contextuality, communication, conjunctivity, communion (in the more explicit sense of Eucharist), and compassion with their respective values of relationship, connectedness, indigenity, attentiveness, balance, thanksgiving, and self-giving love.

COMMITMENT

Certainly, in every seminary community there are seekers. My own experience has borne out this observation over the years. Seekers— meaning here those who are still exploring in hope to discover a vital relationship with God through Jesus Christ—should always be welcome in the community of faith. The seminary, however, is something quite distinct from any of its individual members. The seminary-as-community maintains a radically different stance. Rather than an institution in search of something, it is a community that has been found already. Its life and work are founded upon a faith, both in which and by which it believes.

Anselm of Canterbury was the first to give clear expression to this idea of theology as *fides quaerens intellectum*, i.e., "faith seeking understanding," in his classic work *Cur Deus Homo* (Why Did God Become Human?). In similar fashion, Augustine made it clear that faith precedes understanding because unless you believe, you will not understand. Robert Cushman's comments related to the theological legacy of Duke University Divinity School in his apt title *Faith Seeking Understanding* are appropriate here:

> For me, whatever more it is, at rock bottom, Christian theology is "faith seeking understanding." And the *scandalon* is—as the Apostle Paul first saw and enforced upon the attention of the Corinthians—that appropriating faith in "the glory of God in the face of Jesus Christ," however alien to the wisdom of the world, is just exactly the kind of response suited to that unspeakable gift which passes all human understanding.

For the apostle faith is acceptance of the incomprehensible grace of God in Christ. Accordingly, St. Paul saw that it was indeed a God-given starting point, *from* which, not *to* which, enlightenment proceeds.[5]

All of this is simply to say that theological education begins with commitment. It reflects, in fact, a particular commitment. Theological education in the Wesleyan tradition proceeds from a commitment to Jesus Christ as the Living Word of God to us. The God-given starting point from which we proceed is the received faith tradition of the apostolic community as recorded in Scripture. A part of our unique *paideia* is to be shaped by this particular tradition. Most important, therefore, this peculiar calling is not primarily objective, learning about things or even learning about God; rather, it is primarily relational, knowing God in Christ as we have already been known. If theological education is about a relationship and a matrix of extended relationships, then it will call inevitably for life-shaping decisions. The actions that emerge out of the decisions we make—all within the context of God's grace and love—will create new people and communities of witness and service in the world.

COMMUNITY

All that I have said thus far, in fact, implies a community. Theological education is by definition a corporate endeavor. If John Wesley was correct in his assertion that there is no such thing as a solitary Christian, then it certainly must be right to say that there is no such thing as a solitary theologian or a solitary theologue (as my father called a seminary student, in an earlier generation). I think we are coming to appreciate more fully the ways in which we are shaped by the communities out of which we emerge and in which we participate. It is not that this appreciation is something new, it is simply an increased acknowledgment of our indebtedness to the complex network of relationships in which we live and work. It takes a community to raise a child, we say, but it also takes a community to form a Christian. It takes a community to shape a mature Christian leader in the life of the church.

My experiences as a theological educator in Africa taught me a lot about community. I will never forget one day when my students in Kenya, in a rather playful conversation after class, were deriding Europeans and Americans for the blatant individualism of our cultures. "We believe in community," I argued. "The family, for example, is something of supreme worth in my culture." It was only after a return to my own culture that I realized just how bankrupt my words actually were. I could perceive the radical narcissism of my own culture only as it stood in stark contrast to the other cultures in which I had immersed myself and that lived out of an authentic "I-am-because-we-are" view of the world. Communities not only encourage us to open our eyes, but actually can help us to remove the scales that leave us blind and disabled. This effect is particularly true of those communities in which all the participants do not think the same thoughts, act the same ways, or find the same kinds of worship meaningful. The principle of unity-in-diversity can be a powerful tool that God uses to shape the life of any member, as long as the One that unites is affirmed and the distinctive aspects of each participant are appreciated.

Community is multifaceted. When considered from the biblical standpoint of *koinonia*, it reflects the profound intimacy that Jesus shared with his followers, especially those disciples (both men and women) who gathered around this particular rabbi and were captured by the radical message of *shalom*. The seminary community shares in Christ and his benefits. To be in community means to partake of God's grace, to share the good news, and to live in the promises of Christ. To share with Christ means that, as a people faithful to Christ, we live with, die with, suffer with, are glorified with, are buried with, and are raised with Jesus. Just ponder for a moment what it would mean to be shaped by these realities in the context of theological education. Community also assumes that we share together. We are called to live in fellowship with one another. We live out a partnership with God in the world. Connectedness in all of these dimensions was one of the great hallmarks of the early Methodist movement. Life in the seminary community offers a multitude of opportunities to be connected to Christ and to one another.

CONTEXTUALITY AND COMMUNICATION

There is no such thing as community in the abstract. Each community comes into existence in a particular time and place, with a unique constellation of persons who reflect their own hopes and dreams in life; each community is the product of a particular context. Likewise, people enter into a seminary community from multiple settings and will be sent out to serve in a multiplicity of contexts. *Paideia* takes place, therefore, in a specific context. Moreover, theological education's process itself is shaped by its setting and the various constituencies to which it seeks to be attentive.

Given the plurality of acknowledged contexts in contemporary life, seminaries must equip the servants of God to be able to move fluidly between and among changing contexts. Nothing could be more difficult. Is this difficulty any different, though, from the world in which the apostle Paul found himself, and of which he wrote the following statement?

> For though I am free with respect to all, I have made myself a slave to all, so that I might win more of them. To the Jews I became as a Jew, in order to win Jews. To those under the law I became as one under the law (though I myself am not under the law) so that I might win those under the law. To those outside the law I became as one outside the law (though I am not free from God's law but am under Christ's law) so that I might win those outside the law. To the weak I became weak, so that I might win the weak. I have become all things to all people, that I might by all means save some (1 Corinthians 9:19-22).

The apostle lived in a world no less contextual than our own. Life has always been contextual. We live in a time when attentiveness to these matters is of utmost importance with regard to the proclamation of the gospel.

I find it virtually impossible, therefore, to talk about the context of a situation without saying something simultaneously about the way in which the context gets communicated. The value of indiginity or particularity (the positive dimension of contextuality) is inextricably bound, I believe, with the quality of attentiveness in life (the characteristic of genuine communication). I want to talk about these things together.

The first words in *The Rule of St. Benedict* say to listen. What the great monastic founder had in mind most certainly was a reverent, ready, humble, sensitive listening. He conceived listening as a lifelong process of learning. In a world that is increasingly a cacophony of sounds and unrelenting noise—where silence for many has become a virtual impossibility—I am increasingly convinced that the key to the Christian life is listening. If listening is an act, then attentiveness is the complementary disposition of the soul. Prayer helps to cultivate a spirit of attentiveness. The secret . . . is attentiveness to God and to everything else around you.[6]

Listening, in other words, is the key to our navigating the complex waters of contextuality. Another way to put this thought is to say that the Christian (read as "the seminary" as well) and the context (assuming all the accoutrements of culture as well) must be in conversation with each other or maintain a dialogue together. Developing the skill of listening well is essential to the health of that conversation. Nothing is more important, I believe, for the life of the church in the twenty-first century. Nothing, in fact, may be as important for our very survival. I often wonder if Reuel Howe's amazing insights in *The Miracle of Dialogue* do not speak deeply to the global circumstances in which we now find ourselves:

> Dialogue is indispensable also in the search for truth and here, too, it is a worker of miracles. Unfortunately, many people hold and proclaim what they believe to be true in either an opinionated or defensive way. Religious people, for example, sometimes speak the truth they profess monologically, that is, they hold it exclusively and inwardly as if there was no possible relation between what they believe and what others believe. . . . The monological thinker runs the danger of being prejudiced, intolerant, bigoted, and a persecutor of those who differ from him. The dialogical thinker, on the other hand, is willing to speak out of his convictions to the holders of other convictions with genuine interest in them and with a sense of the possibilities between them.[7]

This was also the way of Jesus: to demonstrate genuine interest for all of God's children by means of attentiveness and to invite others who held great expectations into a relationship with him, often by the way he demonstrated appreciation for the other. Learning how to listen—to listen to God, to the other person, to the circumstances that surround us in life, and to be attentive in all these ways—can be a life-shaping miracle. Concern for context and the way in which we communicate (particularly through listening) are critical to contemporary theological education.

CONJUNCTIVITY

In talking about dialogue and the relationship between the Christian community and the world, I have been using a lot of synthetic language. The Wesleyan theological heritage is a tradition of conjunctivity, i.e., a both/and rather than an either/or way of doing theology.[8] Several couplets from a single hymn by Charles Wesley illustrate this approach:

Let us join ('tis God commands),
Let us join our hearts and hands;

Still forget the things behind,
Follow Christ in heart and mind;

Plead we thus for faith alone,
Faith which by our works is shown.[9]

Note the explicit connection drawn out between hearts and hands, heart and mind, faith and works. Interestingly, all three conjunctions represent polarities that are often torn apart in the life of the church today. Listen to how John Wesley described the way in which faith is expressed by love in the believer's life in *A Plain Account of Genuine Christianity*:

> *Social love*, if it mean the love of our neighbour, is absolutely different from *self-love*, even of the most allowable kind; just as different as the objects at which they point. And yet it is sure, that, if they are under due regulations, each will give additional force to the other, 'till they mix together never to be divided.[10]

There can be no separation of self-love and neighbor-love. The two must be held together.

Many of the Wesleyan conjunctions are directly applicable to theological education, but none is of greater importance than the synthesis of heart and head.[11] Of central concern to the Wesleys was the holistic formation of their followers. No form of *paideia* is more significant today than that which involves the healthy development of hearts and minds fully committed to Christ. Charles Wesley formulated the conjunction in a memorable hymn,

Error and ignorance remove,
    Their blindness both of heart and mind;
Give them the wisdom from above,
    Spotless, and peaceable, and kind;
In knowledge pure their minds renew,
And store with thoughts divinely true.

Unite the pair so long disjoined,
    Knowledge and vital piety:
Learning and holiness combined,
    And truth and love, let all men see

In those whom up to thee we give,
Thine, wholly thine, to die and live.[12]

John Wesley, in his sermon on the "Witness of Our Own Spirit," speaks of the same holistic integration of the follower of Christ:

> We are then simple of heart when the eye of our mind is singly fixed on God; when in all things we aim at God alone, as our God, our portion, our strength, our happiness, our exceeding great reward, our all in time and eternity. This is simplicity: when a steady view, a single intention of promoting [God's] glory, of doing and suffering his blessed will, runs through our whole soul, fills all our heart, and is the constant spring of all our thoughts, desires, and purposes.[13]

For nearly a century, under the shadow of Enlightenment influence, theological seminaries have been primarily concerned about the development of a learned clergy. Unfortunately, this concern for intellectual rigor has often been at the expense of spiritual nurture. However, pastors with large hearts who have received inadequate preparation in the task of thinking theologically will find themselves hard pressed to tackle the complex challenges of our age. What the church is crying out for today are Christian leaders with steady, healthy hearts (well-developed spiritual lives) and keen, discerning minds (well-developed critical skills). The seminary, therefore, is challenged to create an environment in which prayer and worship is honored as the foundation of the Christian life and ministry and in which scholarship and study are viewed as essential disciplines that enrich and guide the church in troubled times. The "what" of Christian *paideia* in the seminary context is integrally connected to the "how" of learning by action. And so, I turn next to the eucharistic dimensions of teaching and learning as a possible paradigm for this holistic vision.

COMMUNION

One of my former colleagues, Sister Joanmarie Smith, wrote a lovely book entitled *Teaching as Eucharist*.[14] In it she explores the art of teaching through the lens of eucharistic action. Expanding the traditional four-fold action embedded within the liturgy of the sacrament, she examines the five verbs: take, thank, bless, break, and give. In these actions she discerns a paradigm for teaching and learning. Writing from the perspective of the Wesleyan tradition—a heritage defined in large measure by its eucharistic spirituality—I find this connection extremely helpful for the framing of our work.

Think for a moment with me about the actions of Eucharist in relation to the process of teaching. First we take into our hands the bread and the wine. This action is full of meaning. The bread is the product of human labor. It represents a widely distributed community of workers, most of whom we will never meet in this life. The bread began with the care of a farmer, but involved progressively the work of the teamster, the skills of the miller and baker, the distributor, all the way down to the local grocery clerk. Likewise, the wine is the product of multiple human hands. To take these elements is to accept God's desire to nourish and sustain us, to feed us with the strength and love of Christ. In our teaching, we take the work of others into our hands in an effort to nourish and strengthen the faith of those who seek to serve God. The biblical texts, the ideas formulated through the centuries, the actions of the Christian community through time, the insights that enable us to care for people in healing ways—we take all of this into our hands. We celebrate the work of many faithful disciples we will never meet in this life. We take and offer up the work of human hands.

Secondly, we thank God by blessing God. We realize that the very actions in which we are involved are possible because of the grace of God. Gratitude is the next important step. We are grateful to God for the wonder of creation, for Jesus who reminds us who we are and to whom we belong and empowers us through the Spirit to reclaim our true identity, for the family of God supporting us and surrounding us in all that we do, and for the reign of love that Christ brought into the world. We remember. This *anamnesis*, though, is a much larger reality than we can begin to express. It is a remembrance in which God brings Christ into the present moment. It is a true divine-human encounter. Through this remembrance, God draws us into Christ and connects us to a creative and redemptive action. Neither our imagination nor wishful thinking produces this mystery in our lives; it happens through the coming of the Holy Spirit in ways that often transcend our understanding. In teaching, we offer our gratitude to God in the very same way. Through the dynamic interaction of the Spirit with the substance of our study and the community of learners, it is not too much to say that God becomes real to us. In the classroom we meet Christ anew through the various theological, historical, and biblical instruments at our disposal.

Thirdly, we break the bread. "The bread that we break," says Paul, "is it not a sharing in the body of Christ? Because there is one bread, we who are many are one body, for we all partake of the one bread" (1 Corinthians 10:16a-17). In the early church, the expression "the breaking of bread" became a shorthand way of referring to the Lord's Supper. In Acts we find this expression used, not to talk about simply eating together, but with specific reference to the sacramental action of the community: "They devoted themselves to the apostles' teaching and fellowship, to the breaking of bread and the prayers" (Acts 2:42). Also, "They broke bread at home and ate their food with glad and generous hearts" (Acts 2:46). Jesus breaks the bread for the purpose of sharing. Receiving the bread not only unites us to the Lord, but also to one another in Him.

Sister Joanmarie's comment is helpful:

> "Break" in this context cannot mean you should break your students. Nor can it mean that you should allow yourself to be broken, or burn out . . . Breaking the bread makes it possible to give each disciple a piece. All share equally in the communion–even if the size of the pieces vary . . . As we meditate on the application of breaking in order that everyone may share, we inevitably think of the necessity of breaking up a subject or topic to make it palatable to our students. Our students do not learn at the same pace or in the same way. We break open our subjects and methods to give everyone another kind of "break."[15]

We pray, as it were, in the words of the hymn, "Break thou the bread of life, dear Lord, to me." ("Break Thou the Bread of Life," written in 1877 by Mary A. Lathbury.)

Finally, we give the elements to the people of God in the same way that Jesus gives himself to us. There is an intimate and obvious connection between the breaking and the giving. The living Word comes to dwell in us. The wonder of it all! And we meet one another in him through the giving. The mutuality that is implied in this giving and receiving is critical as a paradigm related to our teaching and learning. What is given is a gift; and like all gifts, it can be accepted or rejected. The gifts we believe we offer in our teaching can never be coerced, just as love can never be coerced. All is invitation. The posture is that of "leaning in toward the disciple," the learner, and the expression is that of invitation into a marvelous adventure. In this final action—the mystery of giving and receiving—the central meaning of the sacrament as thanksgiving becomes such a matter of celebration.

COMPASSION

Regardless of how deep and well-founded one's commitments or how vital the community, no matter how attentive one might be to the context and the importance of communicating the gospel in winsome ways despite the dynamism of holistic study and formative worship—if compassion is not the consequence of all of our efforts, we have failed. The goal of theological education as *paideia* is God's re-formation of compassion at the center of the believer's life. To learn what it means to be compassionate and to live as a compassionate human being in a suffering world is what this enterprise is all about, when all is said and done. This is to say that all theological education is by definition missiological. It is oriented not toward what I can become, but toward the kind of self-giving love God can restore to my soul and offer freely through me to others. It has to do essentially with the restoration of the image of Christ in a child of God.

If "service to the present age" is our "calling to fulfill" as the inheritors of a Wesleyan vision, then the church and the seminary of the future must be attentive to the world and its needs, active in compassionate service through solidarity with those who suffer, and articulate with regard to the message of hope entrusted to our care.

Several stanzas of John Wesley's lyrical paraphrase of the Lord's Prayer provide the words to express the prayer of our hearts:

Son of thy Sire's eternal love,
　　Take to thyself thy mighty power;
Let all earth's sons thy mercy prove,
　　Let all thy bleeding grace adore.
The triumphs of thy love display,
　　In every heart reign thou alone,
'Till all thy foes confess thy sway,
　　And glory ends what grace begun.

Spirit of grace, and health, and power,
　　Fountain of light and love below,
Abroad thine healing influence shower,
　　O'er all the nations let it flow.
Inflame our hearts with perfect love,
　　In us the work of faith fulfil,
So not heaven's host shall swifter move
　　Than we on earth to do thy will.

Father, 'tis thine each day to yield
   Thy children's wants a fresh supply;
Thou cloth'st the lilies of the field,
   And hearest the young ravens cry.
On thee we cast our care; we live
   Through thee, who know'st our every need;
O feed us with thy grace, and give
   Our souls this day the living bread!

Eternal, spotless Lamb of God,
   Before the world's foundation slain,
Sprinkle us ever with thy blood;
   O cleanse, and keep us ever clean!
To every soul (all praise to thee!)
   Our bowels of compassion move,
And all mankind by this may see
   God is in us—for God is love.[16]

NURTURING THOUGHTFUL FAITH
AND FORMATIVE PLACES
Steve G. W. Moore

What would it mean if, instead of trying to explain the gospel
in terms of our modern scientific culture, we tried to explain
our culture in terms of the gospel?
—Lesslie Newbigin, *Foolishness to the Greeks:*
The Gospel and Western Culture

People, not places, tend to be better indicators of where God is at work. The good news is that God is always at work, choosing to work, quite often, in unexpected places. It may be a barn in rural Palestine or it may be a law office in New York City; it may be a bar in Fargo or a dance class in Beijing. God is not as concerned with geography as with openness of heart. Sometimes that kind of openness even happens in churches or seminaries. Sometimes not. Though the places where God chooses to be present in extraordinarily real ways may not be the type of places that we think of as holy ground, they instantly become so when God shows up.

Therefore, one of the first and most important lessons to learn about Christian formation and cultivating a thoughtful faith is that these things are not primarily a function of place or curricula. This was a hard lesson for the people of Israel to learn, even when they regularly had God dramatically reminding them of this truth. So we should not be surprised that it may take us a while to recognize this rather simple and obvious lesson. Once we recognize it, we can quit expecting books, people, retreats, or institutions to provide that which is already sitting in our backyard. From the moment of that recognition, we are freed from a lot of grumbling and complaining in the wilderness. Places and people are also freed from unreal expectations of being either security or saviors and instead become our companions on life's journey. There are, I would quickly note, places that intentionally do seek to make a space for God. Through faithful prayer and honest searching, individuals and groups of people combine their heart, minds, and souls with such an openness that pleases God.

Sometimes people think it's the words, not the openness, that invites God. We, like those who have gone before us, want to find a way to make God predictable, manageable, and perhaps controllable. Oftentimes the culture of our churches, seminaries, Bible studies, and other institutions is best described as a culture of words—words spoken, words written, words read, words recorded, words pondered. Recognizing that the places where Christians most often gather are worlds of words is one of the essentials in dealing with matters of Christian formation. We must regularly and faithfully ask ourselves, "How can we bridge the chasm between God's Word and our words and lives? How can we transform the words we use about God to become flesh in the way we work, pray, study, relax, and live our daily lives?"

WHAT TO DO ABOUT THE GAP

I know a good theologian who lives badly. He is a broken person who has become quite skilled at hiding his brokenness. He has a reputation as a thoughtful scholar but also as a mean-spirited and vindictive colleague. He attracts students because he wields power and influence, but he wields them like a sword. His personal life is a mess.

I know a bad theologian who lives well. Most consider his ideas unorthodox and, at times, half-baked. But he is also known as a faithful and generous colleague and a reliable friend. He is winsome and inspirational in spite of his bad theology. He, too, attracts students and models collegiality and generosity in his learning community without deference to theological agreement or political position.

We all know people who in part—or in full—could be described like those mentioned. My hunch is that all of us want both to be good theologians and to live well. No one aspires to bad theology or bad living.

In the 2004 U.S. presidential election, we were bombarded with the shocking news that moral values mattered to many voters. Then, for several weeks following, editorials and news talk show commentary suggested in not-so-subtle terms that those who promoted moral values were not so moral in the way they crafted media campaigns, ran elections, or interacted with those around them. Once again, "religious" people were in the media spotlight and did not fare well. Like the proverbial "deer in the headlights," some religious folks found themselves stammering and sputtering when asked to explain the inconsistencies in belief and action, creed and conduct. One thoughtful commentator, after attempting to provide some perspective on voters and the inconsistencies in our culture, finally remarked, "What we have here is a 'gap crisis.' We all have a gap between what we believe and how we live. But if the gap gets too big, it becomes a crisis. And that's where we are!"

TAKE THAT THOUGHT CAPTIVE . . .

Truth be known, we are not the first generation to be concerned with this gap crisis. In every generation this struggle to keep the mind and heart connected has been a familiar one. As John Wesley so aptly reminds us, "A man may be orthodox in every point, he may not only espouse right opinions but zealously defend them against all opposers . . . and still not be authentically religious [i.e., Christian]."[1] Just as the mind can be disconnected from the heart of faith, so can the heart be disconnected from the mind of faith. This last prospect is more characteristic of contemporary Christianity where faith is presented as mere feeling and experience, able to fulfill psychological needs but disconnected from the transformation of timeless truths.

The challenge to unite "the two so oft divided"—vital piety and sound learning—continues to be present with us. Fortunately, God has and will continue to call men and women to lives that embody a marriage between thoughtfulness and prayer. Some of these lives are well-known individuals, such as Augustine, Aquinas, Pascal, Luther, Calvin, Wesley, Catherine Booth, Dorothy Day, and Mother Teresa. Others are not so familiar names to twenty-first century ears. We have much to learn from them all.

One unfamiliar but extraordinarily helpful approach to Christian formation that shapes both heart and mind comes to us from the unlikely place of the Egyptian desert. It was there that Evagrius Ponticus spent his last sixteen years nurturing a life of thought and prayer. Before becoming known as Evagrius the Solitary, he had been mentored by some of the great early theologians (Gregory of Nazianzus, Basil the Great, and Gregory of Nyssa) and served as the archdeacon in Constantinople. He left his prominent theological community and the promise of a bishopric for the desert and an opportunity to focus on thinking theologically about life. From around A.D. 383 until his death in A.D. 399, he wrote about matters of the intellect and spirituality with the clarity and wisdom that make him such a good guide even for us today. Evagrius said that a thought (no matter how good its content) inattentive or unresponsive to God's Word becomes a diversion from God and even a defiance of God. The goal or highest good for the human creature is a convergence of our knowledge of God, prayer with God, and our daily lives. Knowledge that does not lead to or become prayer is, in Evagrius's analysis, demonic spirituality divorced from obedience to God.

Evagrius's is a simple and important distinction, which with a little practice we can learn to make for ourselves. Our normal, everyday lives are as good a place as any to begin making these distinctions. In fact, it is probably the best place to begin doing it, for there is hardly an hour in a day when there is not an occasion in which to exercise these fundamental discernments.

The French have a wonderful phrase, *deformation professionale*, to refer to maladies people are particularly vulnerable to in the course of pursuing given professions. Physicians may become calloused to suffering. Lawyers risk becoming cynical about justice and truth. Those of us who work as a part of Christian institutions and the church are in danger of having the very words we use about God being the things that separate us from God—the most damning deformation of all.

Such a warning echoes the caution of the apostle Paul when he admonished us not to be deceived by the "wisdom of this world" (1 Corinthians 3:19 NIV). We must understand there is no hint of anti-intellectualism in that or any other teaching of Paul. Again and again he reminds his audience of the importance of being thinking, not only feeling, Christians: "We demolish arguments and every pretension that sets itself up against the knowledge of God, and we take captive every thought to make it obedient to Christ" (2 Corinthians 10:5 NIV); "We have the mind of Christ" (1 Corinthians 2:16 NIV); "Do not conform any longer to the pattern of this world, but be transformed by the renewing of your mind" (Romans 12:2 NIV).

Paul also knows that ideas—even when about God, and maybe especially when about God—can all too easily become self-serving and prideful, not to mention Evagrius's bold designation of demonic. If not brought vigorously, regularly, and devoutly before the living God in prayerful obedience, intellectual activity results in disobedience. Obedience cannot happen in individual isolation. Obedience happens best in community and is most effectively accomplished in the midst of a community that worships and studies, questions and prays, argues and plays, engages and encourages one another in the practices of allowing the Word to become flesh in our lives. Such practices require a larger community of faith; men and women scattered throughout the world who seek to "take captive every thought to make it obedient to Christ" and who challenge others to do the same. An adage often attributed to Francis of Assisi reminds us to "Preach the gospel at all times; if necessary, use words." Perhaps an occasional "take that thought captive" scrawled on our screen savers wouldn't be a bad idea either.

Dorothy L. Sayers once suggested, "It is precisely because of the eternity outside time that everything in time becomes valuable and important and meaningful. Therefore, Christianity . . . makes it of urgent importance that everything we do here should be rightly related to what we eternally are."[2] For Sayers, developing a thoughtful faith is not only a task for the present world—she suggests that separating our living and thinking is to do injury to our soul and eternity!

It seems to me that one of the great challenges of life is bringing together what I believe and how I live. There are times when I think it would be a great deal easier if I had some simple steps to follow, some basic exercises to complete, or some fundamental directions to pursue. Fortunately, life doesn't function that way.

Richard Mouw, as he reflects on Thorton Wilder's play *Our Town*, reminds us of the importance of paying closer attention to life as it is happening to us:

> I still remember a few lines from the haunting scene at the end of the play. Emily has died, but she is briefly allowed to observe her family members going about their daily routines. Finally, when she is ready to go to her grave, she turns to the Stage Manager and asks, sobbing: "Do any human beings ever realize life while they live it? Every, every minute?" The Stage Manager quickly replies that they do not, but after a pause, he adds: "The saints and poets, maybe—they do some."[3]

The truth is, we are all called to be saints and poets in the sense that we are called to realize our lives as we live them. That realization is, in part, what we desire in seeking to cultivate a thoughtful faith.

C. S. Lewis gives us a very helpful insight to this point in one of his works, *The Abolition of Man:* "For the wise men of old," writes Lewis, "the cardinal problem had been how to conform the soul to reality . . ."[4] According to this view, human beings are particular kinds of creatures living in a particular kind of world—the meaning of which had been established by God. The pursuit of a well-lived life involved the recognition of the true, the good and beautiful, and the shaping of institutions that would enable and encourage such recognition.

ENCOURAGING FORMATIVE PLACES

What Lewis describes is, in fact, what was on the mind of many early leaders in the New World of North America. One cannot read John Elliot's declaration of 1643, "New England's First Fruits," and remain unmoved by the clarity of the early settlers' commitment to thinking theologically about the formation of the American colonies.

> After God had carried us safe to New England, and we had builded our houses, provided necessaries for our livelihood, rear'd convenient places for God's worship, and settled the civil government: One of the next things we longed for, and looked after, was to advance learning and perpetuate it to posterity, dreading to leave an illiterate ministry to the churches, when our present ministers shall lie in the dirt.[5]

Elliot and this band of New World Christians shared an Old World vision where learning to think theologically about life was foundational to the moral, spiritual, and intellectual leadership of the community. Their view of the world was informed by a particular experience in learning. No fewer than thirty-four of the early settlers had graduated from Emmanuel College at Cambridge University in England. One of these settlers was John Harvard who had graduated from Emmanuel in 1632 and arrived in Massachusetts a few years later.

The first school those early settlers founded would bear John Harvard's name and be the forerunner of the thousands of institutions of higher learning in America today. From the founding of Harvard until the Civil

War, most American colleges were founded by churches. This phenomenon was not surprising, as the church had given birth to higher learning at every stage in the Western world, particularly since the twelfth-century founding of the *universitas* and cathedral schools.

As the new nation grew, so grew the number of colleges that the church would found in order to serve the burgeoning populace. As the new republic matured and industrialization spread, the schools soon broadened their curriculum to include education and training for other professions along with the standard training for ministry that had been the primary focus of the early colleges. By the mid-1800s, publicly funded state colleges were added to the pool of American higher education, further expanding the access to education and further augmenting the curriculum. Interestingly, even many of those early public institutions adopted missions that were religious in nature, and they often looked to the clergy to provide leadership. The need they sought to address was not secular learning but technical, agricultural, and professional training to serve the ever-increasing industrialization of the marketplace.

Even in this growth mode from the 1600s to the 1800s—and even with the Enlightenment that encouraged a split between heart and head, faith and reason—American educators remained clear on their central task and primary responsibility: *the building of students' character*. This shaping of students' character was not nebulously or neutrally moral instruction; it was nearly always understood as specifically *Christian formation*. Matters of faith and doctrine, as well as conduct and lifestyle, were of concern to educators and a responsibility assumed by the educational institutions at all levels.

It was nearly impossible for educators to think about the enterprise of learning outside the framework of Christian faith. Christianity had been the midwife which gave birth both to the democratic spirit of the New World and to the liberal (i.e., broad and deep) education of American universities. Christian theology, once considered the queen of the sciences, provided the foundations and insights necessary for all truth seeking and intellectual investigation. Thinking theologically, then, was necessary for thinking; to think at all meant to think theologically.

The mission of higher education began to change dramatically, however, with the dawning of a new era in the late nineteenth century. By the late 1800s and early 1900s, the universities and other American institutions began to reject their Christian moorings and tethered themselves to the vague foundations of scientific rationalism and moral neutrality. At best, Christian formation became relegated to the sidelines of the academic world; at worst, Christianity itself was viewed as antithetical to learning in any self-respecting college or university and more than a few seminaries and divinity schools.

The exact reasons for this shift are complex. Historian George Marsden describes the changes in his landmark 1994 study, *The Soul of the American University*. Three major factors in American culture precipitated this swing: scientific and technological advances, ideological conflicts, and increasing religious and cultural pluralism.[6]

Lewis is again helpful at this point. "The modern view," he criticizes, "assumes that the problem is how to subdue reality to the wishes of man . . ."[7] In other words, social institutions (such as government, schools, and even religious organizations) exist principally to maximize the freedom of individuals and aid each person in creating his or her own reality.

Across the centuries, the concern of teaching and learning has been for the whole person: spiritual, social, and intellectual. Human wisdom through the ages has understood that intellectual maturation cannot be divorced from spiritual formation and social development. In the Greek academies, Talmudic schools, medieval universities, and in Western institutions of higher education until the twentieth century, the question was not *if* but *when, where,* and *how* the learner's character could be cultivated, molded, and shaped.

Theologian Stanley Hauerwas once wrote that the church does not *have* a social ethic, but rather is a social ethic. If he is right about churches, this fact is equally true for all places that propose to be about learning and teaching. We are not simply wired for data accumulation; we are wired for relationships. We are not simply programmed for function; we are called to be creative stewards in and of the garden.

"If in striving for excellence, we find ourselves in pursuit of control over our own destinies as human beings, seeking to use education as a means to secure ourselves before God, we will have missed the mark entirely," writes Craig Dykstra.[8]

What does it mean to think theologically—to cultivate a thoughtful faith? In short, it means to respond faithfully and persistently to the call to become like Christ. Or, as Paul said to some of his friends:

> So here's what I want you to do, God helping you: Take your everyday, ordinary life—your sleeping, eating, going-to-work, and walking-around life—and place it before God as an offering. Embracing what God does for you is the best thing you can do for him. Don't become so well-

adjusted to your culture that you fit into it without even thinking. Instead, fix your attention on God. You'll be changed from the inside out. Readily recognize what he wants from you, and quickly respond to it. Unlike the culture around you, always dragging you down to its level of immaturity, God brings the best out of you, develops well-formed maturity in you. (Romans 12:1-2 MESSAGE)

New Ways of Thinking About Church Growth

George G. Hunter III

*[T]he resurrection of Christ directs our attention back to
the creation which it vindicates. But we must understand
'creation' not merely as the raw material out of which
the world as we know it is composed, but as the order and
coherence in which it is composed.*
—Oliver O'Donovan, *Resurrection and Moral Order:
An Outline for Evangelical Ethics*

In the 1960s and 1970s, the church growth mini-revolution led by
Donald McGavran introduced (or reintroduced) five significant per-
spectives to the world's churches. First, McGavran helped many
churches recover their main business, which is not merely serving the
members of the gathered churches but reaching pre-Christian people.
McGavran declared, "It is God's will that His Church grow, that His lost
children be found."

Second, he perceived that the chief objective of both evangelism
(within a culture) and mission (across cultures) is not merely to *preach*
the gospel nor to elicit *decisions* from people, but to communicate the
meaning of the gospel and "to make [new] disciples." This objective is

essentially achieved when people experience two significant life changes: they start following Jesus Christ as Lord, and they are incorporated into some community of the body of Christ. These two changes may occur in either order.

Third, McGavran and his church-growth colleagues advanced the *strategy* perspective in world mission. Many mission agencies would no longer blindly perpetuate their traditional activities (such as literacy, education, medicine, and agriculture) in the assumption that, of course, their activities are advancing the Great Commission. Agencies, instead, became clearer about their objectives; more self-critical about whether their activities were achieving those objectives; and more strategic, flexible, and innovative in pursuit of the objectives.

Fourth, McGavran raised the question about "effective evangelism." He observed that in evangelism "we know what *ought* to reach people" (e.g., tract distribution, preaching to people in revivals and crusades, or confronting pre-Christian strangers with a memorized presentation). However, McGavran dared to ask questions such as, "What approaches, methods, and ministries, in what kinds of contexts, *actually* reach people, gather harvests, and make new disciples?"

Fifth, church-growth people employed extensive field research in order to better determine what are effective mission and evangelism approaches. As church-growth field researchers studied hundreds of growing churches in many cultures and interviewed thousands of new converts, the movement was discovering many principles behind the Christian faith's expansion. In time, Christianity's outreach was being formed in unprecedented ways.

Donald McGavran and his growing army of church-growth researchers and leaders discovered that the key term *growth* is not as simple—and its meaning not as self-evident—as first thought. For instance, some church-growth leaders came to sympathize with their critics' charges that not all growth is good, and some growth may even be undesirable. So, for example, it was observed that some growth may be analogous to *fat*, as when a church recruits and welcomes nominal members who are not serious disciples, or when a low expectation church is content with its people dutifully attending church while the pastor circulates as everyone's chaplain. A church, like any body, has a limit to the amount of fat it can drag along and still be healthy.

Furthermore, some growth may be analogous to *malignancy*. This is the case when a liberal church welcomes new members who have not turned from non-Christian gods and worldviews; or when a conservative church welcomes people who confuse beliefs with faith (e.g., nationalism with Christianity), or who live more by a legalistic ethic than a love and justice ethic. A church is severely limited in the amount of malignancy it can carry without jeopardizing the whole body. The acknowledgment that some types of growth are *not* desirable has helped us to become clearer about the types that are desirable.

Early in his reflections, Donald McGavran observed that Christian movements grow in multiple ways. Collaboration between McGavran, Ralph Winter, and Peter Wagner developed the church growth field's most essential and enduring paradigm. Churches essentially grow in four ways: internal growth, expansion growth, extension growth, and bridging growth. While this typology has endured and has proven perennially useful, our understanding of the types has evolved. With experience and reflection, we can now nuance our understandings within the paradigm in more precise and useful ways.

INTERNAL CHURCH GROWTH

In *Understanding Church Growth*, McGavran defined internal growth as an "increase in sub-groups within existing churches, i.e., increase of competent Christians, men and women who know the Bible and practice the Christian faith. They move from marginal to ardent belief."[1] Subsequent writers have expanded on our understanding of internal growth and have generated more alternative terms for this type of growth than for any other type. Alan Tippett preferred terms such as *quality* growth and, especially, *organic* growth. Importing these terms from anthropologist Anthony Wallace, Tippett emphasized the importance of long-term strength and revitalization movements within the churches. Peter Wagner's glossary in *Church Growth: State of the Art* saw internal church growth as individual "Christians growing in their faith and in living out their Christian commitment." He defined the related term, qualitative growth, more corporately as "the collective improvement in Christian commitment and ministry among the members of a given local church."[2]

Some have used internal growth to refer to all the ways in which existing churches become more faithful, compassionate, or powerful churches. In *To Spread the Power: Church Growth in the Wesleyan Spirit*, I suggest that:

Internal growth refers to the growth in depth, quality, or vitality of an already existing congregation. When the nominal members discover the living Christ and begin following him, when the members are more rooted in scripture or more disciplined in prayer, when the people become more loving or empowered, or more attuned to God's will for peace and justice and finding the lost, then the church is experiencing internal growth.[3]

In the 1970s and 1980s, church-growth researchers did not do as much studying and writing on internal growth as they did on expansion, extension, and bridging growth. This is largely because the writers in the church-renewal movement were already addressing this challenge as, more recently, the church health writers also have done. Some church-growth writers take serious issue, however, with the *renewal* and *health* people who seem to advise a church or denomination to become renewed or healthy enough before getting involved in outreach and mission. That prescription ignores the brute fact that one reason why existing churches often lack sufficient health and need renewing is because they have not been reaching out or involving themselves in wider mission. Furthermore, church-growth experts know that nothing renews a lethargic congregation like getting involved in wider mission or receiving a stream of converts entering their ranks.

EXPANSION, EXTENSION, AND BRIDGING GROWTH

A local church experiences expansion church growth when new members enter the church's ranks. McGavran gave this category three strategic subdivisions:

(a) *Biological growth* occurs when the children of church members come up through the ranks and are received or confirmed into the church.

(b) *Transfer growth* occurs when the church receives active Christians into its membership from another church, whether a church of its own denomination or another.

(c) *Conversion growth* occurs when the church receives new Christians from the world.

Since McGavran's time, the usefulness of adding a fourth strategic subdivision has become obvious: (d) *restoration growth*. For decades, the annual statistical report that many churches sent to their judicatory or denominational headquarters included the number of people received into the church's membership "on confession of faith or restored." McGavran once taught us that such umbrella categories conceal about as much as they reveal. If a church reported fifty new members in that category, who was the church really reaching? The category combined three populations: children who joined from the confirmation class; teens and adults who joined from the world and, therefore, represent conversion growth; and people who had previously confessed faith and been involved in churches but then lapsed—often years or decades ago—and who were now returning to life in a church.

In very recent years, the membership form for United Methodist churches asks them to report in one column the number received "on profession of faith" and in the next column the number received "by reaffirmation of faith." So this denomination's churches now specifically count their restored believers who were lapsed for long enough to have no church from which to transfer. The distinction between *conversion* growth and *restoration* growth is strategically important. Conversion growth usually represents effective outreach to people who had little or no Christian memory and no prior personal history of discipleship. With such people, the church cannot assume much prior understanding or residue of Christian insight and must introduce Christianity from scratch. Restoration growth represents effective outreach to people who did have a background of faith to which they could choose to return one day. With these people, the church often can presuppose some background knowledge and experience. Some of their remembered experiences, however, may be negative, i.e., they may remember church as boring or irrelevant. Such people do not usually return to a church that is like the one from which they dropped out. When they return, they typically come expecting a different type of church and a different type of church experience. Both populations will often have to experience "belonging before believing."

Only about 20 percent of the 360,000 churches in the United States are growing by any of the four subdivisions of expansion growth, with 17 percent of all churches growing primarily by biological growth or transfer growth. Two to three percent grow substantially by biological, transfer, and restoration growth. Less than 1 percent of all the churches in the United States grow substantially from conversion growth. As McGavran used to say, "*That* is where we need to put in our emphasis!" If, indeed, many churches are called by the Lord of the Harvest to experience much more expansion growth, and especially conversion expansion growth, then this calling may require some criteria that church leaders can use to hold themselves accountable.

Substantial Expansion Growth

Some churches expand more substantially than others. *Substantial* growth is a church that doubles its membership strength in ten years. In each year of the decade, such a church may average a number of new members that equals 13 percent of the church's current membership tally, while losing 6 percent of its members to death, transfer, and reversion. So, for example, a church that finished last year with one hundred members, receives thirteen new members this year, loses six, and thus experiences a 7 percent net growth. A church averaging 7 percent net growth per year doubles in a decade.

Movemental Expansion Growth

A church that doubles its membership strength in five years is experiencing *movemental* growth. Such a church would receive, in a typical year, at least twenty new members (per one hundred previous members) while still losing about 6 percent of its members to death, transfer, and reversion. A net growth of 14 percent per year essentially doubles the church's membership strength in five years.

These two guidelines for appraising our faithfulness could, of course, change with the context—lower in a very resistant context, higher in a very receptive context.

Apostolic Expansion Growth

Furthermore, the church is experiencing either substantial or movemental growth is also experiencing *apostolic* expansion growth if at least a third of the new members represent either conversion growth or restoration growth, with at least 10 percent of new members representing bona fide conversion growth from the world. One would be tempted to peg that last standard higher, but it is experientially important for churches to set goals they can, with God's help, exceed. In any case, churches that bring in many converts also retain more of their kids, attract more restored Christians, and attract more transfers.

While causal connections are difficult to demonstrate, there are reasons to believe that the church-growth movement's call to prioritize conversion growth has inspired and guided at least half of the churches in the United States now experiencing more conversion growth than before and has prodded many other churches and church leaders toward a more apostolic orientation.

Extension Church Growth

This growth occurs when a local church (or a judicatory or a denomination) plants a new church to reach people that the mother church would like to reach but cannot because they are too far away. The target population may live beyond reasonable traveling distance from the mother church, may represent a subculture or a particular socioeconomic class of people, or may have a language, dialect, or condition (such as an addiction) that would raise invisible barriers that the mother church could not overcome. Traditionally, the mother church (or judicatory) buys some land, underwrites a founding pastor (or, increasingly, a church planting team), deploys some core members from the mother church, and builds a first building. Cities in the United States are now becoming so multicultural, and even multilingual, that much church planting, even in the mother church's own city, is essentially bridging growth (discussed below). Moreover, we now observe many innovative expressions of the extension impulse, such as the multiplication of congregations within existing churches. Many churches in many nations feature a dozen or more congregations in the same church, usually in several liturgical styles and often in several languages.

When the American church-growth movement came along in the 1970s, many mainline denominations had been propagandized into assuming that church planting was no longer effective. So, despite the country's increasing urbanization, mobile populations, and ethnic immigrations, denominations were planting fewer new churches than ever before. The church-growth movement helped to turn that trend around so by the 1980s, most mainline denominations had doubled or tripled their rate of new church plants. Nevertheless, they are still planting much less than half of the new churches they have the opportunity to plant.

Bridging Church Growth

This type of growth occurs when a church sends cross-cultural missionaries across language and cultural barriers to establish or enhance a Christian movement among a population that is very different from the people of the sending church. Historically, cross-cultural missionaries usually traveled great distances to foreign nations, and that pattern continues. As the United States becomes the most multicultural and multilingual nation on earth, however, planting a Christian movement among, say, Latino, Chinese, Russian, Samoan, Tamil, or Hausa people in one's own nation, region, or city involves many of the dynamics of international mission.

Since the 1970s, the church-growth movement has championed the continuing international mission of the nation's churches.[4] Of the earth's approximate thirty thousand people groups, some ten thousand (numbering more than 2 billion people, speaking several thousand languages or mutually unintelligible dialects) still have no indigenous evangelizing church within their ranks. The church executives, therefore, who once called for a moratorium on sending missionaries apparently were not familiar with even these most elementary demographic facts. Nevertheless, many churches were persuaded not to send more colonial-type missionaries who had not adequately distinguished between Christianity and Western civilization and who were driven to impose Western ways and call it Christian mission.

The call today is for more incarnational missionaries who identify with the host cultures and who can work with the people to develop indigenous Christianity. The church-growth movement's achievement in championing the sending of contextually appropriate missionaries is mixed. Overall, with slight fluctuation, the independent mission agencies are sending more and more missionaries while the official mainline denominational agencies are sending fewer and fewer. Rodney Stark, a leading sociologist of religion, explains:

> The liberal American denominations . . . have become essentially irrelevant to the American foreign mission effort. In 1880, the liberals—

Congregationalists, Presbyterians, Methodists, and Episcopalians—provided more than 9 missionaries out of every 10 sent abroad from the United States . . . By 1935, the liberals supplied fewer than half of the American missionaries . . . In 1996, they sent out fewer than 1 out of 20 of those registered with official mission boards.[5]

INTRODUCING "CATALYTIC" CHURCH GROWTH

It may be time for the church-growth field's most useful paradigm to experience some expansion growth. The established four types of church growth, even with the embellishment of the years, do not sufficiently account for much of the church's growth. Two new categories (one of which will be explained here), with the classical four, can help us account for most of that growth. I find myself calling the two new types *catalytic* growth and *proliferation* growth, suggesting that the church grows essentially in six ways:

1. Internal growth
2. Expansion growth
3. Extension growth
4. Bridging growth
5. Catalytic growth
6. Proliferation growth

Catalytic growth refers to a distinctive, powerful, infectious dynamic that we often observe when a church is experiencing movemental growth (doubling in five years) and/or apostolic growth as defined earlier. We usually observe and experience a catalytic dynamic when Christianity is becoming a wider contagious movement. I am employing the term as a metaphor, borrowed from the physical sciences (especially chemistry) in which a catalyst increases the rate of a chemical reaction. So in a crisis, for instance, a surge of adrenaline catalyzes the body for fight or flight, or creatine ingested before resistance exercise catalyzes the body's production of the chemical ATP that powers two or three more bench presses, which catalyzes more muscle growth. From the earliest apostolic movement, something like a catalyst has always been prominent and potent in contagious Christian movements. The dynamic, like internal growth, is more qualitative than quantitative, but it typically results in greatly increased expansion, extension, and bridging growth.

The catalytic principle is often involved as the faith spreads within a family, clan, or peer group. Consider a typical case. A forty-year-old man from a secular and unchurched extended family, long addicted to alcohol, was detoxed and began recovery at Hazelden Clinic in Minnesota. He continued his twelve-step recovery at a halfway house for six months then moved back home. A friend, who had once boozed with him but was now in recovery, invited him to a church in Chicago that features a large sign: "Recovery Spoken Here." The church welcomed him. He felt wanted and at home. In one of the church's twelve-step meetings, he discovered that the Higher Power revealed to him at Hazelden was the Holy Spirit, who now pointed him to Christ, and who reconciled him to God. While he still carried some of the marks of his past, he was so profoundly changed that his family and peers were astonished. They attended his baptismal service and were deeply moved. The church reached out to his family, friends, and peers, and then to some of their family, friends, and peers. Within six months, thirty were baptized as new Christians. When people observe miracles that they cannot deny or account for (except for God), that experience often catalyzes interest, receptivity, or even active seeking.

The indispensable presence of the catalytic factor was in many, if not most, of history's great Christian movements. The apostles knew of the importance of the catalytic factor, as did figures such as Saint Patrick and John Wesley. My thesis suggests that in virtually every society, there is a regular or established population, and there are also fringe populations whom the establishment regard as impossible or hopeless.

In first-century Galilee, for instance, the marginalized and allegedly hopeless populations included lepers, blind people, deaf people, paralytics, and the possessed, as well as tax collectors ("traitors") and zealots. Much of Jesus' visible public ministry was to such populations. This point was not lost on his disciples who became apostles. Many of the apostles reached groups widely regarded as impossible, even so-called barbarian and cannibal, populations. The second-century apostolic traditions tell us that Andrew reached the Scythians, who were widely regarded as more animal than human. Matthew, at the cost of his life, planted the gospel seed in the land of the cannibalistic Anthropophagi. Following Matthew's execution, the king converted and led many of his people into the apostolic faith.

This catalytic principle is expressed differently in various contexts, depending on which people group the establishment assumes to be impossible. In eighteenth-century England, for instance, when the fencing of the land pushed many rural people out of the countryside and the new jobs of the Industrial Revolution pulled them into the cities, the established Church of England launched virtually no mission to the common people that now crowded into the cities. Such people were not considered fit candidates for Christianization. After all, they did not dress like "good church people"; they had never acquired a church etiquette (they would not know when to stand up, or sit down, or kneel); they obviously could not afford to rent a pew; and they were not literate enough to navigate their way through the *Book of Common Prayer*. How could they become Christians?

John Wesley and his compatriots, however, raised up an apostolic and renewal order within the Church of England that came to be known as Methodism. The Methodists launched an apostolic movement among the very population that establishment church leaders considered impossible. Wesley reflected that religion must not go from the greatest to the least, or the power would appear to be of humans. By reaching an allegedly hopeless population, Wesley believed his movement was demonstrating "the wideness of God's mercy."

For decades, Methodism in India cooperated with the trickle-down model of Christian mission. They engaged the Brahmins and other educated elites, believing that if they could win the intelligentsia, the movement would trickle down to the masses. The theory seemed logical and its implementation put missionaries in touch with their educational peers, but Christianity experienced little advancement by that strategy.

In the late nineteenth and early twentieth centuries, however, a Christian movement broke out among some of the lowest untouchable castes. Western church leaders questioned how valid this mass movement could be, considering the people it was reaching. They commissioned J. Wascom Pickett to assemble a team to engage in three years of field research. Pickett's *Christian Mass Movements in India* strongly validated the movement's authenticity, strength, and miracles. He learned the importance of "never judging Christianity by the people it reaches—but judging it instead by the people it produces."

In recent history, a doctoral student in mission at Asbury Theological Seminary has led such a movement. Vasile Talos was the president of the Baptist Union of Romania for ten years in a period that included the late struggles under Communism as well as the first years following Communism's demise. He enrolled in one of Asbury's doctoral programs. One day while reading for the History of Mission course in a carrel in the library, a thought occurred to him: *the Gypsies matter to God.* Vasile had shared a prejudice widely held by Europeans that the Gypsy culture was virtually impenetrable and that they, as a people group would have no receptivity to the good news of Christ. When he returned home, Vasile convinced his denomination on the merits of a mission to Gypsies. Today, there are about ninety Gypsy Baptist congregations in Romania; many cultural Romanians have observed changed lives and changed neighborhoods and have been attracted to a church that cares enough and dares enough to serve Gypsies. By reaching Gypsies, the Baptists have reached more cultural Romanians as well.

The promotional ministries of Roger Armbruster, on the Internet at www.canadaawakening.com and the opening segment of the *Transformations II* video (www.sentinelgroup.org), have alerted much of the Christian world to a Christian movement among the Inuit aboriginal peoples of the North American Arctic. The Inuit (sometimes called Eskimos) number about 125,000 people, scattered in seacoast villages comprised of three hundred to two thousand residents across much of Arctic Canada, Alaska, Greenland, and Russia. The first known seed for their movement was planted in the late nineteenth century when an Inuit shaman, Anwadeeswak believed that a person would one day bring news of a Son of God to the Inuit.

In the late 1920s, the Church Mission Society of the Church of England sent Canon John Turner to Pond Inlet, Canada, as the first missionary to an Inuit people. Anwadeeswak's grandsons recognized the missionary from what they recalled of their grandfather's belief. In the decade before his untimely death, Turner built a solid church in Pond Inlet while planting seeds in neighboring Arctic communities. In time, the Church Mission Society sent missionaries and planted churches in most of the communities of Arctic Canada.

Through the later itineration by Rev. John Spillenaar in the late 1960s to 1980s, the Full Gospel Church also planted many Inuit congregations. Today, David Ellyatt has succeeded Spillenaar in leading the Arctic Missions agency (www.arcticmissions.com), which takes teams of laity into Arctic communities each summer to join indigenous Christians in building or expanding church facilities.

Church growth in both the Anglican and the Full Gospel traditions proceeded slowly until February 1996, when a gospel movement broke out in Pond Inlet (and concurrently in several other communities) and spread within months to many other Inuit communities. In September 2003, I attended a conference at Baker Lake, Canada, of more than three hundred Inuit Christian people from thirty-five communities across Arctic Canada. One purpose of my visit was to test the validity and usefulness of my catalytic growth hypothesis through observations in Baker Lake and interviews with church leaders from other communities.

The Inuit Christian movement substantially fits the catalytic growth paradigm. Indeed, when the movement broke out in Pond Inlet, the news spread to other communities. When Pond Inlet Christians visited and spoke in other communities, interest and outreach was catalyzed in about eighteen Inuit communities across northern Canada. Many non-Inuit Canadians regard Inuits like many Europeans regard Gypsies, so news of an awakening among this population has triggered a wider curiosity.

In Pond Inlet, some 80 percent of the community's people were addicted to a range of substances from alcohol to gasoline fumes; crime, child abuse, spouse abuse, depression, and suicide also scourged the town. Several addicts experienced faith, and the church served as their de facto recovery community. The church reached other addicts who also responded and their families and friends as well. When the sober townspeople saw these people leading new lives, many of them sought the grace with that kind of power. I was told that in more than a dozen of Canada's Arctic communities, this dynamic has catalyzed the growth of at least a few churches.

Many of these Arctic communities have been rather lawless, like the old American West. Wild, violence-prone young men often abuse women and children, fight, and even kill. A young man who spoke one evening at the Baker Lake conference reported that he was the worst such man in his town. When he accepted Christ and a new life, several of his peers followed and other people were so impressed by these obvious miracles in their midst that they too responded. Most of these Arctic communities, I was told, are much safer and more peaceful since the awakening hit town.

Suicide can become epidemic in Arctic communities; some communities lose 1 percent or more of their people to suicide in a given year. The mayor of one community reported that his community experienced one suicide a month for two years. He tried everything he had learned in leadership, management, and human relations training, but the monthly suicides continued "like clockwork." In desperation, he confessed to his church one Sunday morning that he needed the Holy Spirit's power; if he needed the Holy Spirit, many other people in the church did too. The change in him and others catalyzed a revival in the town. The suicide epidemic ceased.

I interviewed five pre-Christian Anglos who worked in Baker Lake in jobs such as teaching, plumbing, and wildlife preservation. Four of the five said they were deeply moved by the changes they had observed in some of the hopeless Inuit people who had become Christians in Baker Lake. Two accepted my invitation to attend one or more of the evening services of the conference. They were moved by what they witnessed, and one has since joined the Anglican church in Baker Lake as a new Christian. On the way home, I interviewed five Anglos in the Winnipeg airport and hotel who had heard of the Inuit awakening. They were very interested in my firsthand report; they responded with exclamations such as, "Who would have ever thought it possible!"

The conversion of unlikely people does not catalyze *all* of the people into receptivity. For instance, I have interviewed people in Romania who felt *less* receptive toward the Baptists now that they serve Gypsies, and one person in Winnipeg's airport said that she would "have nothing to do with a religion that welcomes people like them Eskimos." But some, often many, are catalyzed into seekers, and these are typically the regular people who would be most useful to the Christian movement: people less inhibited, less inclined to cling to any status attached to class or ethnicity, more altruistic in personality, and more inclined to give themselves in kingdom service.

What could catalytic conversion growth mean in the life of Old East Side Church, a composite, prototypical American church stuck in the 1950s, perpetuating mere religious routines every Sunday and occasional religious activities during the week. Old East Side Church is the embodiment of John Wesley's worst nightmare, a church "with the form of religion, but lacking the power." Several pastors in recent years have encouraged Old East Side to move from tradition to mission. In each case, the pastor did the moving. The people of Old East Side need deeply to rub shoulders with some bona fide miracles. If Old East Side ever gets around to reaching out to some impossible people *and* some of those people experience transparent life change, many (perhaps most, but not all) of the church's members would contract apostolic fever!

What to do? The church's leader group needs to pray about it and target an allegedly difficult population for whom some of the members have a heart: such as the hearing impaired, mentally handicapped, gambling addicts, bikers, abused women, men with anger management problems, an ethnic language immigrant population, or any others the leader group could identify. A task force within the larger leader group would then learn all they could about the target population, identify and network with some of their opinion leaders, and collaboratively develop an out-reach ministry that meets some need within the population.

Then they would start inviting them to church, inviting them again (and yet again) to prove that the church really wants them; inviting most the people who appear the most receptive for an invitation. When they receive their first new people, their friends and relatives should be invited, and then their friends and relatives. In God's good time, they will be receiving some people they once never imagined reaching. In God's good time, Old East Side would discover the apostolic secret of church renewal: a steady stream of converts who have just experienced the grace of God would renew the old church more than all the church renewal and church health programs combined. Old East Side Church, for decades a passive dwindling audience, would now resemble an army for the king-dom of God. And the old members who stayed would never long for any good old days.

NOTES

Introduction

1. Dillard, *The Writing Life*, 32.

An Enclave of Resistance

1. Roman Catholic Archbishop of Los Angeles, "Architecture: Overview," 2002–2004. Online at http://www.olacathedral.org/ (December 2, 2004).

2. Ibid.

3. Trotter, "An Enclave of Resistance" sermon.

4. *Peanuts* is licensed and syndicated by United Media.

5. Bonhoeffer, *The Cost of Discipleship*, 252.

6. T. Jackson, "Thoughts Upon Methodism," *The Works of John Wesley*, 13:259.

7. Snyder and Runyon, *Decoding the Church*, 24–25.

8. The narrative was shared by William Oden as opening remarks of the second session of the 1997 United Methodist Dialog on Christian Unity.

9. Quote found in Nicholson Square Church in Edinburgh, Scotland.

10. Schaeffer, *The Great Evangelical Disaster*.

11. Chambers, *My Utmost for His Highest*, July 27.

12. Excerpted from the "Articles of Incorporation" of Asbury Theological Seminary, July 27, 1931.

13. Larson, *Wind and Fire: Living Out the Book of Acts*, 50.

Thinking As an Act of Worship

1. A helpful work regarding these thoughts is Jürgen Goetzmann, "Mind" in *New International Dictionary of New Testament Theology*, ed. Colin Brown (Grand Rapids, Mich.: Zondervan, 1976), 2:618.

2. Oden, *The Word of Life*, vol. 2., 1. Oden includes references from several early-church and reformation writers who taught the same thing in their day.

3. Ibid., xv.

4. See: Merrill Tenny, *Zondervan Pictorial Bible Dictionary* (Grand Rapids, Mich.: Zondervan, 1967), 759–60; Lawrence Richards, *The Word Bible Handbook* (Waco, Tex.: Word, 1982), 124, 734–35.

5. Kinlaw, *The Mind of Christ*, 14.

6. Sire, *Habits of the Mind: Intellectual Life as a Christian Calling*, 122.

7. Neuhaus, "Encountered by the Truth," *First Things*, October 1998, 83.

8. Guinness and Seel, *No God but God*, 30.

9. Quoted in Sire, *Habits of the Mind*, 216.

The Essence of the Gospel

1. Schell, *China: In the People's Republic*, viii.

The Fullness of Learning

1. Hope and Timmel, *Training for Transformation: A Handbook for Community Workers*, 3.

2. Freire, *Pedagogy of the Oppressed*; see chapter 4 in particular, 135–50.

3. The following paragraphs are based in part upon my earlier discussion of this theme in *Recapturing the Wesleys' Vision: An Introduction to the Faith of John and Charles Wesley*, 67–68.

4. Jaeger, *Paideia: The Ideals of Greek Culture*. Cf. his Carl Newell Jackson Lectures of 1960, published as *Early Christianity and Greek Paideia* (Cambridge, Mass.: Belknap Press of Harvard University Press, 1962).

5. Cushman, *Faith Seeking Understanding*, 328.

6. Chilcote, *Changed from Glory into Glory: Praying from Transfiguration to Resurrection*, chapter 3.

7. Howe, *The Miracle of Dialogue*, 9–10.

8. For a larger discussion of this "Wesleyan synthesis," see *Recapturing the Wesleys' Vision*, 15–22 in particular.

9. Hildebrandt and Beckerlegge, eds., *The Works of John Wesley*, vol. 7. *A Collection of Hymns for the Use of the People called Methodists*, 698.

10. John Wesley, *A Plain Account of Genuine Christianity (A Letter to the Reverend Dr. Conyers Middleton)*, 6.1.6 in Thomas Jackson, ed., *The Works of John Wesley*, vol. 10 (London: Wesleyan Methodist Book Room, 1872), 68.

11. The following paragraphs are based, in large measure, upon my fuller discussion of this topic in *Recapturing the Wesleys' Vision*, 69–79.

12. Hildebrandt and Beckerlegge, *The Works of John Wesley*, 643–44.

13. Outler, ed., *The Works of John Wesley*, vol. 1. Sermons I. 1–33, 307.

14. Smith, *Teaching as Eucharist*.

15. Ibid., 55.

16. Hildebrandt and Beckerlegge, *The Works of John Wesley*, 364–65.

Nurturing Thoughtful Faith and Formative Places

1. Burwash, ed. *Wesley's 52 Standard Sermons*.

2. Sayers, *The Mind of the Maker*.

3. Mouw, "In Search of 'Saints and Poets,'" *Fuller Focus* 12.3, Fall 2004, 2.

4. Lewis, *The Abolition of Man*, 119.

5. Winthrop, *History of New England.*

6. Marsden, *The Soul of the American University.*

7. Lewis, 119.

8. Dykstra, *Growing in the Life of Faith: Education and Christian Practices*, 131.

New Ways of Thinking About Church Growth

1. McGavran, *Understanding Church Growth*, 100.

2. Wagner, *Church Growth: State of the Art*, 292, 298.

3. Hunter, *To Spread the Power: Church Growth in the Wesleyan Spirit*, 32.

4. A people group consists of a tribe, community, or collection of people who share a language dialect, cultural experience, and history that sets them apart in a unique way from other races, tribes, or groups of people in their geographic area.

5. Stark, "Efforts to Christianize Europe, 400–2000," *Journal of Contemporary Religion* 16.1, January 2001: 118.

BIBLIOGRAPHY

"Articles of Incorporation" of Asbury Theological Seminary, July 27, 1931.

Bonhoeffer, Dietrich. *The Cost of Discipleship*. New York: Macmillan, 1960.

Burwash, N., ed. *Wesley's 52 Standard Sermons*. Salem, Ohio: Schmul, 1967.

Chambers, Oswald. *My Utmost for His Highest*. New York: Dodd Mead & Co., 1935.

Chilcote, Paul W. *Changed from Glory into Glory: Praying from Transfiguration to Resurrection*. Nashville: Upper Room Books, forthcoming.

————. *Recapturing the Wesleys' Vision: An Introduction to the Faith of John and Charles Wesley*. Downers Grove, Ill.: InterVarsity Press, 2004.

Cushman, Robert E. *Faith Seeking Understanding*. Durham, N.C.: Duke University Press, 1981.

Dillard, Annie. *The Writing Life*. New York: Harper & Row, 1989.

Dykstra, Craig. *Growing in the Life of Faith: Education and Christian Practices*. Louisville, Ky.: Geneva Press, 1999.

Freire, Paulo. *Pedagogy of the Oppressed*, trans. Myra Bergman Ramos. New York: Penguin Books, 1972.

Guinness, Os, and John Seel. *No God but God*. Chicago: Moody Press, 1992.

Hildebrandt, Franz, and Oliver A. Beckerlegge, eds. *The Works of John Wesley*, vol. 7. *A Collection of Hymns for the Use of the People called Methodists*. Oxford: Clarendon Press, 1983.

Hope, Anne, and Sally Timmel. *Training for Transformation: A Handbook for Community Workers*, 3 vols. Gweru, Zimbabwe: Mambo Press, 1984.

Howe, Reuel L. *The Miracle of Dialogue*. New York: Seabury Press, 1963.

Hunter, George G., III. *Radical Outreach: The Recovery of Apostolic Ministry and Evangelism*. Nashville: Abingdon Press, 2003.

————. *To Spread the Power: Church Growth in the Wesleyan Spirit*. Nashville: Abingdon Press, 1987.

Jackson, T., ed. "Thoughts Upon Methodism," *The Works of John Wesley*, 13:259.

Jaeger, Werner. *Paideia: The Ideals of Greek Culture*, 3 vols., trans. Gilbert Highet. New York: Oxford University Press, 1939–1945; cf. his Carl Newell Jackson Lectures of 1960, published as *Early Christianity and Greek Paideia*. Cambridge, Mass.: Belknap Press of Harvard University Press, 1962.

Jenkins, Philip. *Next Christendom*. Oxford: Oxford University Press, 2003.

Jones, E. Stanley. *Christ at the Round Table*. New York, N.Y.: Abingdon Press, 1928.

Kinlaw, Dennis F. *The Mind of Christ*. Nappanee, Ind.: Francis Asbury Press, 1998.

Larson, Bruce. *Wind and Fire: Living Out the Book of Acts.* Dallas, Tex.: Word Publishing Co., 1984.

Lewis, C. S. *The Abolition of Man.* New York: Macmillan, 1947.

McGavran, Donald. *Understanding Church Growth.* Grand Rapids, Mich.: Eerdmans Publishing Co., rev. ed., 1980.

Marsden, George M. *The Soul of the American University.* Oxford: Oxford University Press, 1994.

Mouw, Richard. "In Search of 'Saints and Poets,'" *Fuller Focus* 12.3. Fall 2004.

Neuhaus, Richard John. "Encountered by the Truth," *First Things* (October 1998): 83.

Oden, Thomas C. *The Word of Life,* vol. 2, *Systematic Theology.* San Francisco, Calif.: HarperSanFrancisco, 1989.

Outler, Albert C., ed. *The Works of John Wesley,* vol. 1. Sermons I. 1–33. Nashville: Abingdon Press, 1984.

Pickett, J. Wascom. *Christian Mass Movements in India.* Jubbulpore, India: The Mission Press, 1936.

Robb, Edmund. *The Spirit Who Will Not Be Tamed.* Anderson, Ind.: Bristol House, 1997.

Roman Catholic Archbishop of Los Angeles, "Architecture: Overview," 2002–2004. http://www.olacathedral.org/ (2 December 2004).

Sayers, Dorothy. *The Mind of the Maker.* Westport, Conn.: Greenwood Press, 1971.

Schaeffer, Francis. *The Great Evangelical Disaster.* Westchester, Ill.: Crossway Books, 1984.

Schell, Orville. *In the People's Republic.* New York: Random House, 1977.

Sire, James W. *Habits of the Mind: Intellectual Life as a Christian Calling.* Downers Grove, Ill.: InterVarsity Press, 2000.

Smith, Joanmarie. *Teaching as Eucharist.* Mieola, New York: Resurrection Press, 1999.

Snyder, Howard A., with Daniel V. Runyon, *Decoding the Church.* Grand Rapids, Mich.: Baker Books, 2002.

Stark, Rodney. "Efforts to Christianize Europe, 400–2000," *Journal of Contemporary Religion* 16.1 (January 2001): 118.

Trotter, Mark. "An Enclave of Resistance" (sermon preached at First United Methodist Church, San Diego, Calif., October 5, 1997).

Wagner, C. Peter, ed. *Church Growth: State of the Art.* Wheaton, Ill.: Tyndale House Publishers, 1986.

Wesley, John. *A Plain Account of Genuine Christianity (A Letter to the Reverend Dr. Conyers Middleton),* 6.1.6. in Thomas Jackson, ed., *The Works of John Wesley,* 14 vols. London: Wesley Methodist Book Room, 1872.

Winthrop, John. *History of New England.* New York: Scribners, 1908.